The Woman in White
an Extraordinary Life

Ada Aharoni

GW00470813

The Woman in White / Ada Aharoni

Contact: ada.aharoni06@gmail.com

ISBN 978-1973930693

ADA AHARONI

THE WOMAN IN WHITE

ℭ

AN EXTRAORDINARY LIFE

*In memory of the
Jewish Egyptian community
that is no more
and its excellent hospital
in Alexandria*

CONTENTS

PREFACE

In the book: *The Woman in White: an Extraordinary Life,* Ada Aharoni shares with us the wisdom and experience of Thea Woolf's remarkable life. Thea talks from the heart, she is real and inspiring. This is a book about being a strong, loving and wise woman, living a meaningful life, choosing one's own road, about the power of the word and of the will, and about the power of the love of life and of humanity. Thea is an unforgettable role model who offers precious gems of truth in every chapter.

This fascinating biography of a heroine who has been called: "The Sister Theresa of the Middle East," is not only an exciting and revealing personal account, it is also a kaleidoscope of astonishing events during World War II in Egypt, which gives the reader a sense of having lived important moments in history. It is a book which makes a strong protest against war, it convincingly depicts its destruction, calamities and pain, however, it also instills in us the hope that War can one day be banished from our lives and planet forever.

Ada Aharoni offers us a blend of penetrating insights, poignancy, compassion and artistry in her rendition of Thea's biographical account. What could have been a more tragical period than Sister Thea's Nazi-infested times? And yet Thea shows through her brave actions, centered in the model microcosm of the inter-cultural Jewish Hospital in Alexandria, that a warm, caring attitude makes a great difference in people's lives and is the main hope for peace and harmony.

The close collaboration depicted between Jews and Muslim Egyptians in the Alexandrian community and hospital during World War II, and their vital cooperation in saving together, European Jews from the Holocaust, delineated throughout the book, is a pertinent example of what the relationships between Israelis and Palestinians could be today. If it was possible for Moslems and Jews in the past to live in harmony, collaboration and peace together, it adds hope and assurance that it is possible to do so in the present and in the future

Some of the amazing stories and vignettes related in this book, such as the one about all first-born males in Mena, Egypt, still being named Moussa after the Biblical Moses, to this very day, are so astonishing that it is like suddenly discovering a live Biblical dinosaur. The forerunner feminist stories such as the one related through the eyes of a little girl, in "The Night of the Staircase," as all the other stories in this book, are true and really happened, and they all succeed to weave together a harmonious and charming tapestry of an exquisite and valuable community, which unfortunately, because of the tragedies inflicted by war, has been uprooted and does not exist anymore.

In today's world, especially in the Middle East, it is important to tell the story of the Jewish and Arab collaboration in saving Jews from Nazi Europe, during the Second World War. Ada Aharoni, whose commitment to peace and to humanity are equal to her commitment to Jewish-Arab collaboration and friendship, has done a splendid job. *The Woman in White: An Extraordinary Life*, resonates with the authenticity of the lives and the experiences of the splendid stories narrated in the book. Thea Woolf is rightly honored by Ada Aharoni's narrative. Ada identifies so much with Thea that she writes her biography in the first person.

This is a book for all ages, a book of love for one's fellow human beings and a song to peace. It leaves one with the happy, fulfilled feeling of satisfaction and hope. It is sincere, well written and poignant, and should be read all over the world. It will be loved and cherished by all.

Daniel Walden, editor,
Studies in American Jewish Literature
Pennsylvania State University

INTRODUCTION

While delivering a talk at the Van Leer Institute in Jerusalem on "The Egyptian Jews--an Uprooted Community," I noticed a pleasant faced silver-haired elderly woman in the first row who was crying all the time. After the lecture, I approached her and asked her if she was not feeling well, and was surprised to hear her answer: "Oh no, these are tears of joy and not of sadness, as this is the first time I hear a lecture on the Jews of Egypt." I asked her if she was an Egyptian Jew, and to my amazement she answered that she wasn't, she was a German Jew, and her name was Thea Woolf.

Thea said she was deeply moved by my words and closely identified with what I had related about the Second Exodus of the Jews from Egypt. She was born in Essen, Germany in 1907, but had lived in Alexandria from 1932 until 1947, where she had been the Head Nurse of the surgical department and operating rooms of the Hospital of the Jewish Community. She had been sent there in 1932 by the Jewish

Hospital in Frankfurt for two years, but when her parents wrote to her to remain in Egypt, because of the rise of Hitler, she had remained there for fifteen years, which saved her life during the terrible Nazi period. All through those years, she had taken notes about the many tales of human suffering, as well as of triumph, which happened around her, and which revealed insights into the tumultuous period of World War II in Egypt.

She then took a small notebook out of her bag, and with pleading eyes implored: "Prof. Aharoni, please read it and write a book about it, or else I will just take it to my grave, nobody wants to look at my written notes and it's a great pity as there are important things which have been overlooked by history!" I excused myself politely, and explained that I was busy writing my own book, *"From the Nile to the Jordan,"* and had no time available to start on a new project. Thea's eyes brimmed with tears again, and they started rolling helplessly down her cheeks. This time, her tears came from a deep source of sadness and helplessness. Wanting to stop her tears, I agreed to look at her notes. We then parted, she to her home in Jerusalem, and I back to Haifa, with her notebook in my bag.

On the Haifa bus, I started perusing her notebook, knowing I would not have the time to do so when I returned home to my pressing duties. Her notes were written in poor English but they had a touch of authenticity, with dates, names and places accurately registered. Her notebook started from her youth in Essen during World War I, through World War II in Alexandria, and up to the time she left Egypt and came to Israel starting in 1947.

Suddenly I was arrested by a new revelation I did not know had existed! Several of her reports clearly showed that there had been a Jewish - Arab Egyptian cooperation in saving European Jews from the Nazi Holocaust in Egypt! This was an aspect of history that had never been related before! I read on, and despite Thea's weak English style and syntax, I was fascinated by this unknown historical fact. In addition, as I read on, Thea's magnanimous, honest and humane personality appealed to me and strongly impressed me. I realized that publishing a book revealing the unknown Jewish Egyptian and Muslim Egyptian cooperation on saving Jews from the Nazi Holocaust in Europe, during World War Two, could strengthen the Peace Treaty between Israel and Egypt.

When I reached home, I called Thea and told her I accepted her suggestion to write a book about her experience in Alexandria, on condition that she tried to collect all the information and documents she had concerning her work in the Jewish hospital in Alexandria, and especially concerning the rescue of European Jews, in collaboration with Egyptian officials. She agreed at once, and added cheerfully that now she understood why she had not thrown away her Alexandrian documents and had kept them closely for more than forty years.

An ideal collaboration developed between us. I was born and raised in Egypt, where my family had lived for many centuries, and Thea had immersed herself into Egyptian life. The Jewish community of which I was part, had been in Egypt for more than two thousand and five hundred years, since the Prophet Jeremiah came to Egypt with his followers, as cited in the Holy Bible. There were about a hundred thousand Jews in Egypt in 1948, and today there are just ten old Jewish widows left in the whole of Egypt! I painfully realized, during my many years of research on this exemplary Jewish Egyptian community that had disappeared, that there had actually been a historical: SECOND EXODUS of THE JEWS FROM EGYPT!" The causes of this painful "Second Exodus," had always intrigued me, and my research on the Jewish Hospital in Alexandria and on Thea's experience in Egypt, illuminated new, revealing and exciting aspects. I am glad that the term "Second Exodus of the Jews from Egypt," which I coined is now widely used in historiography.

Thea's notes, letters and documents, as well as her prodigious, accurate and honest memory, were crucial elements in my shaping of the book: "The Woman in White: An Extraordinary Life". I was fascinated by her personality, her deep love of her fellow beings and her strong will to serve humanity. In addition, her generous, independent and strong leadership, impressed me as an excellent role model for women of today and tomorrow, though she herself lived in the past. She was an amazing forerunner of the "new woman," a fascinating, peaceful Joan of Arc, and as she has been called: "The Mother Theresa of the Middle East." During my numerous and exciting interviews with her over the years, I learned to love and admire her for her integrity, her wisdom, her dedication to her career, and her golden heart.

I closely examined Thea's documents and they helped me in providing proofs of essential episodes and facts, which she related to me in our numerous fruitful interviews. The kaleidoscopic events described in the present book, over more than seventy years, lends a sense of having witnessed big and important moments and events in history, as for instance, when we watch from the roof of the Jewish Hospital in Alexandria, together with Thea, part of Rommel's and Montgomery's battle in El Alamein.

The experience of the Second World War in Egypt, and the rescue of Jews from Europe starting in 1933, through the help of the Hospital of the Jewish Community in Alexandria, initiated and directed by Thea Woolf, is the main theme of the book. My many interviews with Thea, her accurate notes, documents and vast correspondence, proved that this major saving project of Jews who fled from the Nazi Holocaust, was effected by the cooperation of official members of the Egyptian authorities, including the police and port officials, as well as the passport office officials, and the train directors.

This important collaboration between Jews and Moslems in Alexandria, to save Jews from the Holocaust, has never been researched or published before. It is important today to reveal this cooperation between Arabs and Jews in the past, when Israel and Egypt are trying to build a solid bridge of peace in the present, after the historical signing of the Peace Treaty between the two countries in 1979. May the spirit of the collaboration in the present, between Israel and Egypt and between Israel and Jordan, since the signing of the Peace Treaty between them, help today to renew and promote peace talks between Israel and the Palestinians, and to soon bring a complete, lasting and fruitful peace in the whole of the Middle East.

In the present book, *The Woman in White: An Extraordinary Life,* heroic, poignant real-life stories are narrated of attempts by individuals to hang onto their human dignity. Thea helps them to do so, and her stories are complimented by extraordinary accounts of triumph, success and hope. In addition to Thea's stories, I added some of the real-life accounts which I had gathered from my family and friends, and we decided to relate them through the mouths of various patients at the Jewish Hospital in Alexandria, as some of them had indeed been Thea's patients.

These fascinating events, stories and vignettes in the book, add new angles to the climatic cultural tapestry of those tumultuous and colorful times. "The Turkish Prince" depicts the personal story of my brave and courageous grandmother, Regina, in Port Said, who endangered her life by eloping, rather than agree to marry the Turkish prince who had fallen in love with her, and wanted to marry her and add her to his harem of thirty women. "The Certificate" is a story which was related to me by the late Mrs. Flora Matalon; this episode occurred at the beginning of the century and describes the typical love of Zion in the hearts of the Egyptian Jews, even in that early period. "Night of the Staircase" was related to me by my mother, Fortunee Yadid. My Aunt, Becky Mizan, related to me the full episode about a Nazi spy who married a Jewish girl in Alexandria as a cover for his activities.

Many books have been published about the Jewish experiences in Nazi Europe during the Second World War, but very few about Jews in the Arab countries during that period.

It is to be hoped that the present book will be a modest contribution toward filling a small niche in this wide gap. Though the Jewish community in Egypt is no more, it can still provide a living, charming and fetching example of what our global village could be, for as Isaac Bashevis Singer so well said: "In literature as in dreams, there is no death."

Ada Aharoni
July, 2017

"No more war"
Anwar Sadat

"Enough tears, enough blood"
Yitzhak Rabin

A WOMAN OF PEACE

REVEALING REVIEW BY JUDITH BARA

'The Woman in White: an Extraordinary Life'
by *Ada Aharoni*

This work by Egyptian-born author Ada Aharoni, is one of the latest in her long and distinguished career as a University Professor, Author, Poet and Activist. It relates and conceptualizes the remarkable story of the Jewish Hospital in Alexandria, and its Head Nurse, Sister Thea Wolf, a German Jewish Nurse who came to work in Egypt before the outbreak of World War 2 and thus survived the unspeakable horrors of the Nazi Holocaust. However, this remarkable book is much more than this, for it also shows that it is possible for Jew and Moslem, and Arab and European, to co-operate in what is the most important project known to us as human beings - the saving of life, especially under duress.

As such, the book has a resonance for today's tumultuous world where peace is so difficult to bring about, especially in the context of the terror attacks on innocent citizens and travelers whether in New York, Paris, London, Jerusalem, Brussels, Egypt, and in the Far East

This excellent book combines biography, *reportage* and literature. There are three important factors that have helped to make this a very special work. Firstly, from an early age Thea Wolf kept meticulous records and notes relating to her experiences. Together with the help of Ada, she endeavored to find out what had happened to the many people she saved from Nazi Europe, through the Hospital in Alexandria. These notes proved invaluable to writer Ada Aharoni, who in turn became personally enmeshed in this project and was instrumental in discovering the fate of some of those in whose rescue Thea Wolf had participated. Secondly, the fact that the author herself was born in Egypt and spent her early, formative years there, provides a deeper understanding of the nature of that society. This is also a huge benefit to her parallel peace research project - showing how it is possible for Jews and Arabs to co-operate, even under difficult circumstances. Thirdly, the rapport that obviously developed between Ada Aharoni and Thea Wolf was such that each could bring out the each other's strengths and this enriched the work tremendously.

As a child, Thea overcame privations brought about by Germany's defeat in the First World War, and then fought prejudice from her community in terms of training as a nurse. When she had the chance to serve at the Jewish Community Hospital in Alexandria, her family was aghast, but once again her strength of character prevailed and she left, never to return to her family home. The Nazis exterminated her whole family, of seventy-two people, apart from three distant relatives.

The Hospital although primarily established for the benefit of the flourishing Jewish Community of Alexandria, never refused a patient it could help, irrespective of their background. It had a beautiful motto: *"Don't tell me who you are - tell me where it hurts."* Egyptians were treated and employed at the hospital and their friends and relatives were treated there on equal terms. When Jews fleeing Europe began arriving in Egypt, many Egyptian officials, who had the good experience of the hospital in Alexandria, came to enlist to help Sister Thea and her colleagues. From 1937, in conjunction with sympathetic locals and kind-hearted officials, three groups were formed: in Cairo, Alexandria and Port Said, in order to try and help people fleeing from Europe. In many cases, the authorities were persuaded by Thea, to allow them to disembark and stay in Egypt.

A number of daring, brave and risky ventures were engineered by Thea Wolf and her colleagues, with the help of compassionate Egyptian officials, which led to the survival of many people. Not least among these was her own temporary evacuation on the eve of the Battle of El Alamein. The local people involved in these escapes participated genuinely for humanitarian reasons, and differences of politics, religion and culture were set aside. This surely is a lesson that could serve as an example for today, in terms of bringing together Moslems, Jews and Christians.

Thea Wolf remained in Alexandria until 1947, when she

decided to move to Palestine. This decision was based on her idea of 'owing it' to her family and to all those who had died in the Holocaust, to establish a safe haven for survivors and for future Jewish generations. Accordingly, Thea left Egypt and in April 1947, and she started work as a nurse in a government hospital in Tiberias. After the United Nations voted for the partition of Palestine, she was urged by her many Egyptian friends to return to Egypt for her own 'safety' - even by the Egyptian embassy in Jerusalem - as it was inevitable that war would break out after the British left Palestine in May 1948. In the event it was not the Jews of Palestine who were forced into exile, but unfortunately, the Jews of Egypt, many of whom were expelled from Egypt after the establishment of the State of Israel.

Thea eventually settled in Jerusalem and engaged in voluntary work to promote peace. She lived to see the beginnings of peace between Israel and her beloved Egypt, and the Signing of the Peace Treaty by President Sadat and Menachem Begin, and she prayed that this would be taken to its ultimate conclusion - Israel living normally and in peace alongside all her neighbors in the region, including the Palestinians. Regrettably this process has suffered several setbacks, but Thea's example shows us that we should never give up hope or cease working towards this aim. Let us ensure that like Thea, our lives are not lived in vain in this regard.

Thea Wolf (born in 1907) passed away on the 14th of April, 2005, in Frankfurt on Maine, at the hospital where she studied to become a nurse.

Judith Bara London, England

Dr. Judith Bara is a lecturer in Political Science at the University of London, and a British literary critic.

ACKNOWLEDGMENTS

I am deeply grateful to all the friends, colleagues and family members who have collaborated in bringing precious information and special gems to this special book. I am especially grateful to my departed Haim, for his wise, deep and loving comments. Haim proved to me throughout the writing of this book, that happiness is to be married to one's best friend.

I am deeply grateful to Professor Daniel Walden, for having read the manuscript so thoroughly and with such sympathetic eyes, during my sabbatical at Penn State University. Special thanks are also due to Grace Steele for her accurate and friendly insights. I also want to thank my two dear friends Liliane Dammond and Tahita Hadar, for their warm hospitality which enabled me to establish contacts and continue my research during my stays in New York.

Special thanks go to Georgia Jones, my inspiring and efficient first publisher in California, who like Thea, believes in the message of *Not Living in Vain*.

Ada Aharoni
Haifa, Israel

1

NOT IN VAIN

As early as I can remember, it was quite clear to me that I myself was solely responsible for my life. In my young years, I took pride in that private bit of knowledge. I felt personally honored that I knew something many adults did not seem to know. My parents were very kind and loved me in their manner, but what could they know about my real inner aspirations? Later on, I opened my eyes and ears still wider, and saw that people often blamed fate for their own passiveness or mistakes. I decided I would try my best not to be guilty of this unwise sin toward myself. However, the one thing I was most afraid of, was to live my life in vain.

I looked around with young, keen eyes, and did not like what I saw: wars, human suffering, disease and starvation. The world seemed to me the most absurd of all times. What could one frail person like me, do to alleviate, to repair, to bring about a better, happier world? Where does one begin?

After much pondering, I decided to follow the Jewish saying, maintaining that if a person could save even just one life, it would be as if she had saved a whole world. And I chose to become a nurse. I had no inkling then of what the future lay in store for me--the strange events, and the numerous lives that would call on me pleadingly from distant, dark graves.

My decision to become a nurse was a great shock for my parents. It was as if I had decided to become a sort of nun, renouncing a normal young girl's life. What they would have liked was for me to be like other girls: to enter a boarding school for a year or two, in order to learn "good behavior," embroidery, dancing and cooking, and later to marry a respectable young Jewish man. That was what my parents and everybody else considered to be "the normal way of life." But I wanted to do more than that with my life. The world was full of pain, sickness and calamity. I wanted to help. Where could I be of more help than in a hospital? How could I just dance and cook when there was so much misery around? In a time where parents held full sway and control of their children's lives, the pressure upon me to yield to them was tremendous.

"An intelligent, beautiful and talented girl like you will be wasted in a hospital," my mother wept. I loved my mother, but I realized that it was under those very circumstances that my strength must be in evidence.

"I will be wasting my 'embroidery life' if I stay away from the hospital," I said. When they saw how determined I was, they eventually let me go. Today, however, I realize that although I didn't agree with my parents then, I am deeply grateful to them, because the seeds for my whole set of values and way of life were planted deep in me, in my parents' home.

In April 1927, my Aunt Rosa accompanied me to the Congregation of Jewish Nurses in Frankfurt on Main, on 85 Bernheimer Landwehr Strasse. It was to become my home for the next five years. For the first two years I was to be a student nurse, and if I succeeded in passing the tough German government examinations, I would become a registered nurse.

Sister Johanna--an elderly nurse, in charge of the entry room, the phone center, and operating the automatic main gate of the building--accompanied me. I sat down in the waiting room for newcomers and felt some kind of holy silence during the few minutes I had to wait before being received by our "Mother Superior," Sara Adelsheimer. I was shy and very impressed by this tough queen of the new empire I had just entered. She kindly welcomed me and introduced me to Sister Dora, who was in charge of the nurses' home. Dora smiled at me and accompanied me to my room on the third floor, which I shared with two other student nurses for the next two years. The room was neat, sunny and pleasant, and I suddenly felt a wave of well-being enveloping me. Both my mind and heart told me I had made the right decision.

The gong rang for lunch, and we had our meal downstairs in a large dining room. There I had the pleasure to be introduced to old Mother Superior Minna, who was the founder of the Congregation of Jewish Nurses in Germany before World War One. I was awed by her serious look and her kind, sensitive face, which still bore traces of the once tough matron. I was also introduced to the staff of Head Nurses. All of them were wearing golden brooches, which meant they had twenty-five years of service. I was impressed by their various imposing personalities, and the orderly atmosphere. I easily found my table, where a napkin was already prepared on the table with my name and number. This little item and bit of attention made me feel at once welcome and wanted.

"This is Thea Wolf, the new student nurse who has come to us from Essen," Sister Dora said, her blue eyes twinkling all the while. I blushed under the fixed stares, but then realized that despite their apparent toughness, the nurses' faces were smiling at me, and I sat down in relief. I was not an outsider anymore, I was part of the family.

After lunch, all the nurses went up to their rooms for a rest. I did the same, but couldn't rest, so I started to unpack my suitcases and to arrange my belongings in the closet. I wrote a letter to my parents telling them that everything went well and that I felt fine. At supper, the nurses at my table tried to make me feel at home. The conversation was lively and interesting, and all new to me. I felt I was about to tread into an exciting and vivid new world; the one I had chosen among all other possible ones as best befitting my pursuits in life, and my main goal of not wasting my life in vain. The nurses told me that the lights in our rooms had to be turned off at ten o'clock, as we all had to be up at five o'clock in the morning in order to be on duty at six at the Hospital of the Jewish Community in Gagernstrasse. We had only to cross a well-kept, blossoming garden, and to open the door leading to the hospital area. I did not like the idea of waking up at five o'clock, every morning, for the next two years of my life, but this was part of my being a nurse, and I had to get used to the idea.

I couldn't sleep on that first memorable night. I looked back at my former sheltered life at home, and tried to analyze the deep motives for my decision to become a nurse, in spite of my parents' disapproval. I wanted to reassure myself that I had made the right choice. For my own sense of self and for the mission to help humankind which I felt I had to accomplish, I decided with rectitude in being the thing I had chosen to be. However, I was somewhat afraid to become tough and authoritative like some of the elderly nurses I had met. I warned myself, on that very first night, to prize my tenderness and be able to display it at appropriate times so as to avoid becoming a mirror of those who value power above life and love.

Some of my earliest memories begin with the outbreak of World War One. My father was called to fulfill his duty towards the German "Fatherland" from the very beginning of the war in 1914 until its end in 1918. He served in France, then in Russia, and again in France. The thanks he received for his good services during the First World War, was to be deported to the abominable Lodz concentration camp during World War Two, together with my mother, sister, and her four-year-old son. I never saw any of them again. Sixty-eight other members of our family were also sent to various concentration camps: Lodz, Auschwitz, Bergen-Belzen, and Maidanek. All of them died there--seventy-two talented, loved and loving human beings.

But on that first night at the hospital, when strips of my life flipped like a backward video film, I didn't have an inkling of the dreadful times ahead of us. I was just an earnest and keen explorer on the brink of a new continent, to which I yearned to give all my youthful enthusiasm, my vital energy and my exuberant love of humanity. I would be tough, tender, cheerful, live a long life, and make my patients healthy, so that they too would live long happy lives. I felt I was a "woman-knight," a tiny Joan-of-Arc who, armed with courage, willpower and dedication, would surely celebrate the victory of living a full and meaningful life, not only for herself but also for humanity. "Have a green life, Thea," I blessed myself, "but give it back to the world, fully blossoming..."

The Synagogue in Essen burnt down by the Nazis - full of Jews at prayer

2

STREET CHILD

World War One ended. Kaiser Wilhelm abdicated and went into exile to the Netherlands. The German army was in complete disorder, and in our town the revolutionary party the *Spartakists* ruled. For a long time, food was rare; there was no milk, fruit, butter, meat or vegetables. Everything was rationed. We were always hungry, and the four of us literally became street children who stole raw potatoes from vans to quiet the pangs of our hunger.

On one of these tumultuous days mother heard that at the butcher shop of the Krupp Factory one could buy sausages made from horsemeat. I was eleven then, my sister Alice nine, and my cousins Elsa seven, and Hans just four. We got a few pennies from my mother who said, "Now you all go to the butcher shop, stand in the row with the other people, but don't talk to each other; behave as if you do not know each other, so that each of you will get a piece of sausage."

She hesitated a moment, then bit her lip and added, "the fact that the sausage is not kosher doesn't matter. You eat it on the street, and hopefully God will pardon us for this sin, because you are very hungry and God pities starving children." So, we went to the Krupp butcher shop, and we silently stood in line.

Suddenly windows were broken and people shouted, "children first for their sausages, children first..."

We were suddenly pushed to the front of the row, and received our horse meat sausages. When we wanted to pay for the sausage, the woman manager cried, "Oh, no! This is a present from the revolution."

I quickly gobbled my non-kosher revolutionary sausage ravenously, thanking the generous "revolution" in my heart. So did my starving sister and little cousins, and we went back home and returned the money to mother. She became angry and said, "You should have paid for it! You should never again accept anything from the revolution, because this revolution is only theft and disorder!"

So, we all solemnly promised never to accept any gift from the revolution again. Even four-year-old Hans promised, "I will never, never in all my life receive *any* gift from *any* revolution." He pouted and mother smiled. When we saw her beautiful smile, we all smiled in relief. I was glad, because lately, mother was always sad and worried. Our father had not yet come back from the front, whereas other fathers from the neighborhood were already at home. She feared something terrible might have happened to him. We children still spent most of our days in the streets, as schools were still closed.

We were yet "street children," in every sense of the word, including the dreadful hunger that ripped our stomachs at every hour of the day and night. Poor mother did her best for us, but had no more money and no work. Even if she had money, there was nothing to buy. This is when I started

hating wars. Why can't war be killed? I asked myself.

One late afternoon a soldier with a long beard, suddenly approached my sister and me and said, "Good afternoon, Thea, good day, Alice. How are you children?"

We looked at him and whispered to each other, "Who is this soldier? How does he know our names?" We decided not to talk to him, as mother told us never to talk to strangers and we ran away.

Later when we returned home, we saw through the window of our kitchen the same soldier sitting beside my mother on the couch. We were frightened and thought he had come to arrest mother because we had eaten unpaid non-kosher revolutionary horse-sausages. We all ran away quickly to our Aunt Paula.

"Tante Paula," I cried, "there is a strange soldier in our home sitting with mother in our kitchen! He even knew our names! Does he want to arrest us for eating revolutionary sausages?"

Our Aunt Paula, her husband Sally, as well as their two daughters all laughed at us.

"The soldier is your father, Thea," Aunt Paula said joyfully. "He finally managed to come back home from the war."

I was amazed; I still couldn't believe her story. For to us our father was just a picture on the wall in our dining room.

Though we had written greetings on postcards to him during his four absent years as a soldier in France and Russia, I had an unexplained feeling he would never come back. My sister too shared that feeling. We were so afraid to go back home, that we were allowed to stay at our Aunt Paula's house for a few days.

One day the same man, this time in civilian clothes, came to see us. We closely looked at him, and at the chocolate cigars he offered us, and finally decided that the man was indeed our father, because he had always brought us chocolate cigars before the war. We took the cigars shyly but happily. This time we did not run away, but just stood there blinking in disbelief and joy. We even let him kiss each one of us, and I had tears in my eyes when he hugged me.

"Now please come back home with me, children, mother is waiting for you," he said in a deep voice, which I at last recognized as my father's. And we proudly went back home arm in arm with father, our real flesh and blood father and not just a picture on the wall. I hated war still more for having stolen our father from us for four long, desolate years.

Fifteen members of our family served in the German army during World War One; four of them died a "hero's death," and their widows got cold silver medals instead of live, warm husbands. The other eleven live "heroes," like my father, were murdered in the Nazi concentration camps in World War Two, by the same people who gave them the silver medals in World War One.

My mother's brother Fritz was one of the four men who didn't come back from the war. He was the first soldier from his birthplace in Argenschwang near Bad-Kreuznach, who died a war hero's death, and his picture is still chiseled in the War Memorial of the little village. Since his wife died before World War One began, Uncle Fritz's children, my cousins, Elsa and Hans, were orphans and were living with us.

Fortunately, my own father came back from the war and started to work immediately.

He was a butcher, but business was still very bad. Our butcher shop had been closed during the war, and my mother had to manage with the little money she had left, until it all disappeared, together with the cows and sheep that were confiscated by the army. Even after the war food was still rare, and yet we children had to take with us every day not only our own piece of bread to school, but also a second piece for poor and hungry comrades.

We had a cousin by the name of Gerta, who was born retarded. She had great difficulties in walking and talking. We had to pay her a visit at least once a week, and each time we could afford it, we brought her something special, a chocolate, sweets, or a piece of cake. Mother always said, "Don't ever forget the poor, the miserable, and the sick!" The poor, the needy, and the sick, became part of my earliest memories and deepest consciousness.

Our house was situated on one of the main, busy, commercial streets of Essen. Most of the workers of the big Krupp war industry complex, as well as the coal miners, lived near that part of the town. We often asked our parents to leave the working-class quarter and to move to a more comfortable one. But our parents always gave us the same answer, "If we move away from here, we shall forget the poor. We should never forget them and always try to soothe their burden." Remembering their words, makes me feel that the seeds for my wanting to become a nurse and alleviate the sores of humanity were most probably sown then.

For the Jewish holidays, we children were accustomed to getting new clothes and shoes. But before receiving the new garments, we had to decide what coat, dress, shirt, and whatever else we were ready to give to the poor of our neighborhood. I must confess we did it with great pleasure, knowing that we would get new clothes.

After the war, I was glad to go to school again. I liked going to school, which was a nine-year preparatory school for teachers. After having passed the school's final examinations with honors, I bowed to my parents' wish that I should go to the "high commercial school." After completing my studies there, at the age of sixteen, I got a job as an accountant in a wholesale factory. I stayed there for two years, but did not feel I was doing what I wanted. I felt strange and uninvolved. Then suddenly the wholesale factory went bankrupt, and it permitted me to quit without feeling I let anybody down. What I really wanted was to be in contact with human beings and to help them in some way or other.

I had already acquired some experience in aiding people when after the end

of the First World War, Jewish refugees from Poland arrived and settled in our town The Jewish community, as well as the different Jewish youth organizations, started to take charge of these immigrants, whom we considered as our brothers and sisters. I also took part in these activities; it gave me a wonderful feeling of doing a *mitzvah*.[1] I was not wasting my life; I was being of use to others and helping to the best of my abilities. My parents did not approve of my activities, which often took me out of doors late into the night. Though they protested, I persisted, knowing I was doing something important--I was helping human beings who needed my help.

"These Polish Jews are known to be dirty, disorderly, and unruly," my mother cried in exasperation, "I don't want my daughter to have anything to do with them!"

"Human beings are more alike than not alike!" I argued. "The only difference is that some are more fortunate than others...."

Every time I returned from these philanthropic activities, I had to go up to our maid, Liza, who had a little apartment on the top floor, and she helped me to clean myself and to change clothes. My mother wanted to make sure I brought no Polish words, microbes or vermin home. But when she started to argue with me, saying that instead of wasting my time with "these low people and matters" I should start preparing my trousseau for my future household, I could not remain silent.

"Being exposed to another language and culture," I told her, "increases the perception that the world is populated by people whose philosophy is other than ours, and this can perhaps prevent bigotry. Mother, you always taught me

1   Mitzvah: Hebrew for good deed.

that all people cry, laugh, eat, and die, and that links us all together...."

"But those Poles could wash more often!" she retorted.

My father often took my side. He explained to her that I belonged to another generation. "These young people have a different outlook concerning their way of life," he argued, "so let her do what she wants. In any case, she isn't doing anything wrong, and maybe, she's doing something right!"

I could have kissed my father then. He understood me. He knew that for me material values were unimportant. What was important were the human and spiritual values, to help people and try to make this world a better place for all of us.

3

GIVING

As I had lost my job, I decided to start on a new career which was more to my liking. With the help of a good friend of mine, a social worker by the name of Bertha Heyman, I got a job as a housekeeper in Berlin at the Orphanage of the Jewish Women's Organization. My decision caused turmoil at home. My father had to calm my mother down, as well as the rest of the family. All my well-meaning uncles and aunts were aghast at my decision. In their eyes, I was a black sheep because I had decided to leave my family circle, and to travel to Berlin on my own, something which was unheard of for a girl in those days. But I traveled to Berlin anyhow, despite all the protests, and worked as a helper in the orphanage for eleven months. The pay was very small, but I was more eager to give than to receive.

The orphanage was located at first in Berlin-Schoenberg. Later we moved to Herms Dorf on 10 Albrecht Strasse. Miss

Ida Heinrich, the headmistress, was in her fifties; she was efficient and accurate, but rather stern and dry. She instructed me minutely about my duties. I was to get up every morning at six o'clock in the morning to start the central heating, as it was during the wintertime; put coal into the oven; light the fire in the kitchen; clean the carpets on the steps by hand with sauerkraut, which was supposed to do wonders; then prepare breakfast for the twenty-six orphans. All were girls, from the age of six to twenty. They all came from destitute Jewish families or broken homes. They all had problems, but there was nobody in charge of their psyches or inner lives. The orphanage catered to their bodies but not to their souls. When I gently alluded about that to Ida, she rudely responded: "This is none of your business!" But I had already learnt from my experience as an accountant that the judicious response to a gibe can disarm the rude person, removing the power to injure. So, I just said: "It is indeed none of my business, but only yours, and I am sure you will take care of it." But she didn't.

I had to wake the children at six o'clock, then see they went to the bathrooms, then to the washrooms, then to the dining room without talking. Only whispering was allowed because at that time the headmistress was still asleep. I had to wake her up at seven o'clock. She came out of her room at seven-thirty, said good morning to the children, and then returned to her room, where I had to serve her breakfast. Then she left her room, and I had half an hour to clean it. After I finished cleaning it, I had to call her for inspection. She put her right middle finger between her eyes, always looked at the same picture on the wall, and said, "Little Wolf, please straighten the picture one millimeter more to the left," or sometimes, "more to the right." The same conversation was repeated every day. Apart from that, nothing. She was a silent headmistress, and her icy silence kept us all on our toes.

In the meantime, all the children left for school. I then had to clean the whole house and prepare the meager lunch for the children, who returned from school around one o'clock. They had to clean their hands and faces, then they sat down at the table together with the headmistress and me. They didn't dare talk. After having finished lunch, they started their homework. At around six o'clock in the afternoon they helped me to set the dinner table. We had bread, jam, and some kind of porridge. I don't remember having given them fruit or a piece of cake more than once a week. The budget of the orphanage was very small. Once a week a man came to take the dirty linen away and bring the clean back; and once a month a seamstress came to repair clothes.

I only had half a day off on Saturdays. The headmistress left the orphanage on Sundays, and returned in the evening. My bed was in the sickroom; there were always one or two sick children there with me, and I had to look after them during the night. The children were grateful to me for trying to be a mother to them. Perhaps my taste for looking after sick people was sharpened during this period. I found out at that time that among its other benefits, giving of oneself fulfills and liberates the soul of the giver who is as enriched as is the recipient.

The children were allowed to visit their families only once a month, and their families could come and visit them also just once a month. It was a bleak and orderly world where everyone knew her duty and her place. Not everyone took advantage of these regulations; many girls preferred to stay at the orphanage, and only a few family members showed up to see their children. But the children never complained, and they never asked to be returned to their parents or relatives. I also cannot remember a social worker ever coming to talk to the headmistress, to me, or to the children. And yet, despite all the deficiencies I was aware of, my world was enriched by the experience I was getting, and more important, I felt that intangible but real psychic force of good in the world, increasing. If they were not catered for at the orphanage these children would roam the streets, I reflected.

The headmistress went once a month to the Jewish Community Center in order to discuss current matters concerning the orphanage. The two ladies who were in charge of the economic problems of the orphanage and donated most of the necessary money came now and then for a short visit. Then the children had to stand in line, curtsey, and say thank you for everything. I can't remember that the children ever got any sweets or any warm words from the two ladies, who seemed somewhat ashamed of their charity and benevolence. I pondered their behavior and realized that they felt that not only was it degrading to accept charity, but it was equally degrading and debasing to give it! I was astounded at the revelation. I like charitable people and like people who have generous hearts and giving natures--people who are capable of being a friend to anyone in need. Why, I pondered, did those two benefactors, as well as the headmistress, not feel as I did? In their desire to distance themselves from the recipients of their largess, they exiled themselves from their gifts and were completely estranged from the objects of their generosity.

Little by little I began to look at things from a still more critical point of view. "What does it do to the souls of the children when they have to constantly curtsey and thank bitter and dry women for the meager bread they eat?" I asked myself. I remembered the young girl Gerda, my predecessor, who left the day after my arrival. She had said to me then, "In time you will learn a lot here. Much more than you bargained for!" And I did. But I felt that I was casting my bread upon the waters, and was so glad when I saw the joyful faces of the children who benefited from my actions and my love. The children to whom I read beautiful stories before they went to sleep, showed me their overflowing gratitude by telling me their dreams about them the next day. I felt that each individual dream strengthened the pillars of their personalities and private worlds.

There was only one young girl by the name of Ilse, who was eighteen years old, in whom the headmistress took a personal interest. Towards all the others she had a cold attitude. Her answer to me whenever I made any suggestions to make the institution a warmer place, was, "Don't worry, the children are happy here!"

"Are they?" I asked myself uneasily.

I got attached to the children, and tried to do what I

thought was good for them. They were delighted by the special attention I gave each one of them, and they all liked me, but I tried not to have any preferences. This was quite a hard task, as each one of them wanted me as her special friend, protector, and substitute mother. I indeed felt as a mother to all of them; they were all my children.

One of the sad events that occurred at the orphanage, comes back to my mind. We got a new arrival, a six-year-old girl by the name of Lonzy, the child of a drunken father and a drunken mother. They had five other children, who were all admitted to other Jewish orphanages. Admittance day was on Sunday, and happily only a few children were at home that day. Lonzy arrived accompanied by her mother. She was not drunk then and had brought an old suitcase with her, saying that Lonzy's clothes were in it. The mother left the orphanage quickly, and Lonzy immediately started to cry; she wanted to go home. What could I do in order to calm her? She didn't want to eat or play she only wanted to go back home, and she wailed her eyes out for hours on end. It was pathetic to watch, and I felt utterly helpless. I almost sat down myself to weep at her side.

I decided to take her to her room and to open the suitcase her mother had brought. Maybe, when she saw her own familiar clothes and toys placed in order in her new closet this would quiet her. So, I opened the suitcase. Lonzy wept and wailed still louder. To my surprise a horrible smell came out of the suitcase--a sharp, acrid smell of urine and excrement. There were no clothes, but only rags

soaked with filth! I closed the suitcase quickly, and

suddenly Lonzy stopped crying. The cat was out of the bag. She looked at me with large, imploring, and apologetic eyes, still wet from her profuse tears. It was as if she were saying, "I am ashamed for my mother, but it isn't my fault." She knew all along what was in the suitcase and had been deeply frustrated about what my reaction would be.

I hugged her, and reassured her. "Oh, I'm sure, your mother took the wrong suitcase; this must be your father's suitcase!" Lonzy nodded her head in relief. Her father was a rag picker. "Next time, when your mother comes to visit you, she will surely bring your clothes." I smiled at her.

The little girl nodded again, and her big shiny eyes cleared. Lonzy at length fell asleep. But after that, she became very sick with pneumonia for several weeks. I nursed her all the time. She was an affectionate child, and an intelligent and obedient patient. Sometimes, late at night, I couldn't loosen my hand from her quivering fingers when they clung to mine like a drowning soul clutching a saving raft. When she at length left her bed, she seemed to have forgotten everything. Her mother didn't show up at all, and Lonzy didn't ask to be sent back home. Her mother had simply been ashamed to bring her daughter to us without clothes; because she didn't have anything she decided to bring a suitcase with what she had--urinated rags! She didn't realize that her sensitive child was watching and what this would do to her.

At the end of the eleventh month of work at the orphanage, it was clear to me that I couldn't learn anything more from my work there, and I couldn't change anything, as much as I tried. I had to leave the place and choose my future profession. I decided then and there to enter a nursing school. I had often had the opportunity of accompanying some of our children to the Children's Hospital in Berlin, and I liked the atmosphere and fell in love with the profession. This was a world that spoke to my heart; and it suited my personality and aspirations. Here I could do something worthwhile--I would not live in vain. I decided to make an application to the Congregation of Jewish Nurses in Frankfurt on Main, because it was known to be the best institution of its kind. I informed the headmistress of the orphanage about my intention. She didn't say anything; she was accustomed that her helpers didn't stay there for longer than a year. She pursed her lips in bitter silence, and I was glad to leave her icy room for the last time.

I said good-bye to the children the night before I left, and hugged each one of them warmly. They were sorry but not too surprised; they too seemed to be accustomed to the changes of personnel. When I closed the door of the orphanage behind me, I took a deep breath. The air seemed at once purer, and I felt liberated. On my voyage back home by train, which lasted ten hours, I promised myself to remain in contact with all the children. The letters I sent them later were never answered. Maybe they didn't even get them? Maybe they did, but could not afford the stamps to answer them? Maybe the headmistress threw them all away?

Whatever the reason, I was saddened by the fact that I had lost contact with them. The headmistress Ida, to whom I had also sent a letter of thanks, wished me all the best on a picture postcard of the orphanage, but not a word about the children or my letters to them. Later, I learned that she got married to a widower, but continued to manage the orphanage. Did he have a softening influence on her? I hope so, for the children's sake, and for his and her sake.

I was glad to find father and mother at the railway station where they came to greet me. I had informed them already about my decision to become a nurse; I needed their consent, because I was still a minor, and I knew they were not happy about my choice. However, when they met me at the station, mother told me that she went to ask our rabbi's opinion, as she respected him very much. She related that he had told her, "You have to be proud of your daughter, because she is the first Jewish girl in our community to choose to study nursing which is an elevated and noble profession, and she will probably be the only one for a long time!" So both mother and father finally, reluctantly agreed to sign their consent. However, later they changed their minds, and became proud of their "nurse daughter," who passed her examinations with honors, and became Head Nurse in charge of the operating rooms.

Thus, I succeeded to step from the road which seemed to have been paved for me and cut myself a brand-new path. Each of us women, just as much as men, has the right and the responsibility to assess and choose the road which lies ahead. Nobody can know our nature and our desires more or as well as we do. We need to carefully gather our resolve, and carrying only the necessary baggage, courageously step off from that set road into our new chosen direction, which is as in the Hebrew saying; "the bird of our soul" - *Tsipor ha-Nephesh.*

In his wise tale about what women really want, Chaucer teaches his penitent Knight that what a woman wants is "the mastery" to make her decisions about her own life. That first night in Nurse Land, I already felt I had reached "the mastery" over my own being, and that it opened a flashing "open sesame" road before my exhilarated eyes.

4

NURSELAND

I must have fallen asleep after all. Suddenly the floor bell rang; everybody was out of bed. I too, quickly jumped up. I had to be at the seamstress's room at eight o'clock and to take my three nurse's garments. The seamstress had to examine them to check if they were made according to the regulations, especially the distance from the edge of the apron to the ground. It had to be seventeen centimeters from the floor. I also had to bring along three white aprons, a black coat, and a black veil. The heels of my shoes had to be low, and the dark stockings had to be plain. Modern, short-cut hair was forbidden, and so the length of my hair was checked too.

When all my clothing was found to conform to the regulations, I was sent to the Mother Superior, who was the only one allowed to fix my student's brooch on my starched collar for the first time. After the pinning of my brooch, she folded her haughty looks and put them in the drawer. She then told me a few sentences which I have remembered and tried to follow all my life: "Thea, my advice to you as a novice nurse, is to carefully watch the steady march of the human parade. Good manners, tolerance and dedication are the highest manifestations of a good nurse and a lofty human being. Attention must be paid not only to what is said but how it is said; listen to the music behind the words. Pay attention not only to what you wear, but also how you wear it. In fact, you should be aware of all we do and of how we do all that we do...." Wise words from a wise and experienced person, words which have clung as tasty clusters of ripe grapes to my cells, all my life.

When I was accompanied to my first ward, the Chirurgical Men's Ward at the Hospital of the Jewish Community, I immediately took a liking to the ward; everything seemed essential and important in it. The doctors and nurses were "repairing" human beings, in literal terms, and it fired my imagination. They did what the seamstress was doing in her shop: cutting the worn parts out and sewing everything anew. In my mind, I sat quickly again on Joan of Arc's steed, but this time it was for healing and not for fighting. Thus, from my very first day on, I liked to work in chirurgical wards, and especially under the wise and capable eyes of our excellent Chief Surgeon--Dr. Fritz Katz.

Our workday started every morning at six o'clock, and lunch was at one o'clock at the nurses' home. We had to be on duty again at three o'clock until seven in the evening. Dinner was also in the dining room of the nurses' home, and it was always accompanied by lively and stimulating conversation and exchanges concerning the experiences of our day and I thirstily drank in every word. Work was everything to me then; I died with every dying patient and was reborn with every recovered one. Whenever one of our young patients died, especially children, I was angry with God. How could he be so cruel? How could he take away a budding life that had just started to blossom? Why was his grip around the throat of some of his victims so slow, and around that of others so swift and merciless? "Why and how do you make your choices, O God?" I cried in despair. "Why rob such young lives?" I always managed to make my peace with God at the end, though my questions remained unanswered and they continued to baffle me.

Night service began at seven o'clock in the evening and ended at seven o'clock the next morning. This went on for three weeks. We had an afternoon off every week, and a full day off only once a month. Our theoretical medical courses were given to us by the doctors. The lessons began promptly after duty at the wards. We were constantly tired from the work and from the lessons and very often slept during our half-day off. New courses started twice a year, and on the whole, we enjoyed them. We were overworked but contented and fulfilled.

Despite the rigorous conditions, we young nurses were always cheerful and in good humor, and the patients loved us. We distributed the parcels and the sweets we got from home among ourselves and the patients. In summertime, we went to our luscious fruit orchard, full of delicious apples and peaches, which was adjacent to the hospital, and picked the mellow fruit from the trees, which we relished in secret. I must say, they had a very special, forbidden taste--even tastier than Eve's apple!

We got attached to the different wards we were sent to during our two years of study, and we did everything to improve the rooms and the large patient halls. We put flowers everywhere and dainty napkins on the bed tables. On Friday evenings, we lit candles and perfectly cleaned the washrooms and the door latches, as they all had to glitter brightly for the Sabbath. On the Sabbath, we conformed to the required rules of rest and tranquility. We did not write down temperatures then, nor did we clean the bed tables, nor put on the lights. We enjoyed the change, as all young people do, and brightly welcomed the coming of the Sabbath queen, every week, with a beautiful rose or camellia flower from our garden for each of the patients.

One of the things we young students especially liked on the Sabbath were the delicious cakes the patients got for dessert at lunchtime. There was always a large variety and more than enough cakes, so that we nurses, could get an extra piece in the kitchen ward, if nobody saw us. That, too had the special taste of the forbidden. The kitchen maids were our cronies and saw to it that we always got our coveted slices of apple strudel or plum pie. I still relish their melting taste on my tongue and in my palate.

The Jewish nurses were highly esteemed in Frankfurt especially by the neighborhood around the hospital. We knew most of the families, because they liked to be treated at our hospital. We were usually friendly and enjoyed laughter, and we knew how to communicate our happiness and *joie de vivre* to others. Wherever we went, to shops or to the market, or to the theater, we were not allowed to go out in civilian clothes; we had to wear our prim, starched snowy white nurse's uniform. Even later, as registered nurses, we had to ask for special permission to wear civilian clothes.

When we walked about in our uniforms, everywhere people greeted us appreciatively in the streets, even those who did not know us personally. Even the tramway conductors to the hospital and the nurses' home, knew us and greeted us joyfully whenever we entered the tramway. The good feeling that life was worthwhile and an exciting adventure accompanied me throughout that period. I remember a large inscription on the wall of our students' hall which read: *"Eine Schweitzer ist da um zu dienen, und nicht um zu verdienen."* *"A Nurse Has to Serve and Not to Deserve."* We were all eager to serve.

Graduation day arrived, and we proudly received our diplomas. The imposing Mother Superior congratulated us and admitted that we had all worked hard for it. I felt it was indeed so, but that she could have made a warmer speech. I still remember her warm words of advice when she pinned the brooch on my uniform two years before, and thirsted for more of her wisdom and experience. Having passed with flying colors the Governmental Health Department tough exams, after our graduation we were upgraded and were each put in charge of a certain part of a ward. We were also in charge of the practical instruction of the new students, and we gladly tried to pass on our knowledge and experience to them.

Our salary was low, just enough for pocket money. But we were contented, as material things were never important to us. We had all the advantages of living in nicely furnished rooms, with all the then available commodities and meals, clothing and vacation money. We had two vacation weeks at the beginning, then three weeks and ultimately four weeks a year. Most of us didn't aspire to any change in our material standard of life, what we got was more than enough. Dedication to the profession was our inborn need and our main goal in life, all else seemed unimportant. We were not going to be helpless spectators in front of human pain. We had taken a firm stand by its bedside and were fighting against our destructive enemy day and night. When we won, this was reward enough in itself. Our thoughts were altruistic, our hearts pure, and we gave our whole vitality and energy to our work, asking for nothing in return but to be of help to humanity and to those under our care. Our efforts were admired by patients and doctors alike, and nobody dared to belittle our devotion and our enduring patience and goodwill.

I was at length promoted to Surgical Nurse and worked for nearly two years in the operating rooms under Dr. Katz, and the reign and stern eye of Bertha, the staunch, dry and impeccable Head Nurse. I liked the work which seemed to me so vital, and learned something new every day. It was the first time, so I was told, that Bertha tolerated the same nurse beside her for more than a year, and I was proud of it. Every time she scowled darkly at me, I flashed my best smile at her, and it worked.

However, I never knew the real reason she liked me. Perhaps because I was so eager to learn? Even the doctors were in fear of her. She and 'Rosa Narcosis,' as she was nicknamed, the Head Nurse of the entire Surgery Department, who was also in charge of her department for more than twenty-five years, were usually on no-speaking terms. To Bertha's dismay, Rosa was also in charge of administering anesthesia to the patients, either chloroform, ether, or chloroethyl, which were in use at that time. No surgeon would have dared to start the operation before he got the okay from Rosa. Narcosis was not only a responsible duty, but a holy rite; and we all watched Rosa spellbound, including the dismayed Bertha, who considered it a breach of her authority and an intrusion of the "enemy" into her domain. But even the mighty Bertha had to bow down before the still mightier Rosa Narcosis. I smiled at both, and they respected and appreciated me probably because of my ardor and zeal, and perhaps also in an indirect way, because of my cheerfulness and good humor.

I was on duty most Saturdays. Often Bertha came to tell me bluntly, just ten minutes before I was to leave the operating room for off-duty, "Today you can't have your half-day off."

"But I have been working for three consecutive Saturdays," I would protest inwardly in despair, not daring to utter my choking words aloud. But she often read it on my face, despite my bent head, drooping shoulders, and sheepish smile.

"If you want to be a nurse for as long a time as I have been, and succeed in your work" she said bluntly, " then you will also have to deal one day with your subordinates the way

I behave towards you, and that's it. There's no other way...."

I never contradicted her. I reluctantly took a book or a newspaper and sat back on the chair of duty. The nurses from the various other wards sometimes came in for a few minutes to sympathize with me, and told me I should protest. But I knew that one-day Bertha would come to say thank you for everything, and to notify me, "You are now on your own, tomorrow you start a new job." So, I tried to accept my burden without too much disappointment, and waited patiently for the announcement that would promote me and free me to fly with my own wings on unknown, new, stupendous healing waves.

Later, the day when the Nazi deportation orders came for all the Jewish nurses who were still working at the hospital, this brave nurse Bertha killed herself with a poison injection, rather than fall into the hands of the Nazi murderers. Most of the nurses who were deported to the concentration camps had been adorned with high honorary decorations for their great service in the German army during World War One, but this did not deter Hitler's slaughterers. This is how the Nazi regime repaid them for their service to their Homeland. None of them returned from the abominable concentration camps--they were all exterminated.

On one of those Saturdays when I was on duty, nurse Hilda, who was a good friend of mine came to tell me a secret. She had heard that the Jewish community in Alexandria in Egypt, had sent a request to the Congregation of Jewish Nurses in Frankfurt for a Surgical Nurse who could also take charge for a certain period of the Nurses' School and be Head Nurse of the newly constructed Hospital of the Jewish Community there. She whispered excitedly, "I just heard that Mother Superior will propose that you should take this job for two years! What do you say, Thea?"

I was amazed and delighted on hearing the news. The challenge fired my imagination, and the exotic setting of distant Alexandria, on the shores of the azure blue Mediterranean, added to the charm. I had for some time played with the idea of studying something new, but this enchanting opportunity had never crossed my mind. I had indeed considered asking the Mother Superior to give me a job outside the hospital, something where I could feel more responsible; some of our nurses were attached to stimulating social municipal posts; and I thought that with some luck, I could be nominated for one of them. But this job in Alexandria was still more responsible and exciting than anything I had imagined! So, when the Committee of the Congregation of Jewish Nurses in Frankfurt, after having consulted me, agreed together with the Mother Superior to "lend me out" for two years to the faraway community on the shores of the Mediterranean, I was very excited, happy and enthusiastic. I again had to put before my parents a *fait accompli* knowing how hard it would be to convince them to let me go. It was like a bombshell to them.

"What do you know of Egypt and their Jews?" my mother cried out in exasperation and despair. "It's a backward and primitive land, and you will be very out of place and unhappy there!"

"It's a very weighty decision you're making, Thea," my

father said anxiously, with a heavy heart and a worried look
in his eyes. But they both knew me well by then. Once I had
made a decision which seemed to me to be the right one,
there was no moving me. I was exhilarated and felt I was
another Dr. Livingstone or Alfred Schweitzer, on the brink of
discovering a new continent, and bringing modern medicine
to a new part of Africa. My parents came to talk to me again
at the hospital and to meet the future chief surgeon of the
Jewish Hospital in Alexandria, our extremely capable Dr.
Fritz Katz. "Promise us to consider Thea like your own sister,"
my father begged him, "and not only your surgical nurse."
Dr. Katz measured them with an amused look in his eyes
and nodded his head in agreement. He kept his promise to
the very end, he was a responsible big brother towards me
whenever I needed him, and never abused my confidence
in him. But even after he had promised, my parents tried to
convince me not to go. They told me they were sure that the
hospital in Alexandria was in reality just a tent, and that the
few remaining Egyptian Jews, probably lived in dirty mud
houses or tents too, like the Bedouins, surrounded by sand
and camels and dangerous sandstorms that would blow me
away forever. "There are probably no streets, trams or buses
in Egypt! How will you manage, dear little Thea?" my mother
cried in despair. "How will you get to the Hospital?" she
asked.

"Probably by bus, as everyone else," I answered her,
smiling reassuringly, and kissed her cheek spontaneously.

"What bus?" she cried, "there are only camels over there,
I tell you!" she wailed in despair. "A camel will come to the

door of your tent at dawn to bring you over the desert to the hospital caravan, poor, poor Thea...."

When she saw that I was not affected by the material calamities she described, she tried another line of argument: "What is the great idea of going back to Egypt where in Biblical times the Jews were slaves in bondage? Don't you remember we were liberated and taken out of Egypt by Moses?" she asked tearfully; "which means," she continued, "that God doesn't want us to be there! It's a sin! "she added. "Why do you want to go back there today, Thea? The Jews there, if there are any real ones left, are surely like Arabs, and probably are still treated as slaves." She had bitter tears in her eyes and it pained me to hurt her.

My poor, bewildered father added, "Your mother is right. It's all a vast, uncivilized desert out there, and the people are so backward and so poor! How will you manage, my little Thea? Please think of us and how we would worry about you, and reconsider your choice."

"My daughter wants to be a slave..." my mother sobbed.

In my parents' eyes, it was as if I was proposing to turn the wheel of time two thousand years back! How wrong my mother and father were. In Alexandria I found a modern, civilized, flourishing city, bustling with life and local color. The Jewish community there was a cultivated, well-organized, advanced and wealthy one, and they received me like one of their own daughters. How in the world could my parents guess then that I would stay alive, throughout the horrible Holocaust, just because I decided to go to Alexandria?

"Thea, please promise us that you will always wear your nurse's uniform," my mother pleaded tearfully, as if the uniform were a talisman which could save me from all harm. But I saw how important it was to her to hold on to something even as trivial as that, and I promised my parents that for at least one year I would always wear my nurse's uniform, even on private outings. I assured them that I would always be grateful to them for the gift of life which they had given me, and that I would always use it for honorable purposes. They were still not assured, but with tears in their eyes and in their hearts, they finally let me go.

"Yes, yes, I will not accept any invitation from people I do not know well," I promised just before I left, "and will likewise promptly return to Frankfurt and Essen, after the two years of my coveted, willing 'exile in the Land of Egypt.'"

Destiny decided otherwise. I stayed there for fifteen years, and it saved my life. I wish I could have taken them with me, it would have saved their lives too. How strange but true, that one of the best places for a Jew during the Nazi period was in an Arab country. My dear parents' memory, as well as that of my beloved sister, cruelly murdered by the Nazi killers, never leaves me. I feel their presence in me the instant I shut my eyes, to this very day. It is their initial abundant care and love which they bestowed upon me in my youth, which has given me a power larger than myself. In later years, this initial inner strength and human values instilled in me by my parents, allowed me to venture into the unknown and to accomplish things that were beyond me.

Sister Thea Wolf

5

THE JEWISH HOSPITAL IN ALEXANDRIA

Thus, in 1932 after I had been a nurse for five years at the Hospital of the Jewish Community in Frankfurt on Main, I was sent on assignment as head nurse and surgical nurse to the newly opened Jewish Hospital in Alexandria, founded by a wealthy Egyptian Jew by the name of Baron Behor de Menashe. The Jewish Community in Alexandria was estimated at 40,000 people at the time they founded the hospital. In all, there were about 100,000 Jews in Egypt then. The official numbers registered by the Jewish Community, I was told, showed less as not all Jews were keen to be registered and paid members. The new hospital was up-to-date and well equipped, and it was designed by a famous Italian architect in the grand "palazzo" style. It contained one hundred and seventy beds and was staffed by Jews, Moslems, Christians and Copts, who had studied either in England, Germany,

France, America, Egypt, or Lebanon.

The hospital was open to people from all creeds and cultures. Those people who were unable to pay were treated free. Patients even came from abroad, as it acquired the reputation of being the best hospital in the whole of the Middle East. During the Second World War, it served the Allied troops based in the region, and was highly commended for its services.

On my arrival in Alexandria, I was warmly received by Mr. Josef Aghion, the president of the Jewish community then. The German consul, too, was at the port of Alexandria to greet Dr. Katz and me; at that time, there was a small but active German colony. Members were either big cotton dealers or bank managers and head clerks at the branch of the Dresden Bank. They used to send their patients to our hospital, until that sad day when all the German Jews had to get a "J" (Jew) stamped on their passports, according to the newly issued anti-Semitic Nazi regulations. Even during the official visit of the German destroyer Emden to the Port of Alexandria, in 1937, we still operated on two of the sailors for acute appendicitis and they thanked us profusely for our dedicated and expert treatment. After the stamping of the J's, we decided their racism was unacceptable and they were not worth being cared for. We turned them away without any qualms, and they were forced to go to the state hospitals which did not have the same high standard which we had.

My first impression of Alexandria was very favorable. I was surrounded by warm, generous, understanding, bright and helpful people. I strangely felt as if I had known them for a long time, and as if many of them were my own aunts and uncles. Their doors were opened for me from the first moment we met; and not only the Jews, but also the Egyptians, Americans, Greeks, Italians, French, English, and Armenians. Several of these kind people whom I met, told me that they were ready to help us for whatever we needed for the hospital. From the very beginning they made me feel as if I had never left home, both at the hospital and in the town. They were familiar, but not intrusive, exciting and stimulating yet affable, and they tried to help me fulfill my new duties in the best possible way. Naturally, this friendly atmosphere helped me enormously in attaining my aim, which was to make the hospital in Alexandria a model of the Jewish Hospital in Frankfurt, in all ways: the organization of the general medical staff, of the nurses, the aides to the nurses, the cleaning workers, the kitchen staff, the linen department, and the laundry. I asked first of all for the construction of a home for the nurses. My request was presented to the board of the Jewish community of Alexandria that sponsored the hospital, and happily it was immediately accepted. The nurses' home was built on the hospital compound. It was a modern, spacious, elegant and comfortable building which we were all proud of.

At the beginning, we had six fully graduated nurses, who all came from Germany; but four of them later left for Palestine. All the other nursing staff were mostly Alexandrian Jews; but we also had some Arab, Greek, Italian, and French nurses. Some of them had no previous experience, and I and the doctors had to instruct them in practical nursing and also in theoretical knowledge. I explained to them that my main concern was for them to be always helpful, and attentive to the wishes or the complaints of the patients, and asked them to report to me if anything was amiss. I also trained them to be on time for duty, to dress neatly, to prepare the meal trays with attention and love, and also how to feel the pulse, to take temperatures, to prepare the patient for treatment or for an operation, and to prepare the beds accordingly. That is, I had to instruct them in all the basic rudiments of what makes a good nurse. I do not remember that I ever met with indifference or contradictions. The nurses loved and respected me, and it was wonderful to feel that I was creating an entirely new and efficient staff. Something living and vibrant which did not exist before and which was born and growing under my touch. I felt the weight of the responsibilities heaping upon my frail shoulders, but the sense of wonder and extraordinary fulfillment strengthened me. I shared my burdens with others and they became as vigilant and enthusiastic as I was. A few of the foreign nurses inter- married with Egyptian Jews, but they usually continued to work at the hospital, as we all felt deeply involved and attached to our work. Most of the nurses stayed with us from the opening of the hospital until its sad enforced closing by the Nasser regime in 1960.

The climate of goodwill and comradeship was the general atmosphere in all the wards; as for instance in the wards for internal medicine, where Lotte Fleck, a nurse from Germany, who was a good friend of mine, was in charge. The same atmosphere reigned likewise in the gynecology department which was run by Dr. Dora, an excellent Egyptian Jewish doctor. It included a busy delivery ward, where Marie, the midwife, was in charge. She was a Jew from the town of Kerson, who had left Russia at the beginning of the revolution in 1917. She was an extremely experienced midwife, highly regarded, liked by all, and very devoted to her profession. She was also the midwife for the aristocratic upper class and the Royal Court of King Farouk, and delivered his children, including Princess Ferial, daughter of his beautiful first wife Farida, whom he later divorced. The reason he gave was that she only bore girls! King Farouk was not aware that it was the male who determined the sex of the child, and not the woman. Unfortunately, many people in the Middle East and elsewhere, are still not aware of this medical fact to this very day. Dr. Katz tried to explain this in his special humorous manner to the unhappy peasants who became *Abul Banat*, the "Father of Girls," which was a derogatory appellation for fathers who did not have sons, and who often wanted to leave their newly-born daughters at the Hospital.

"When you plant potatoes, what do you get?" Dr. Katz asked Ahmed, a farmer and an unhappy new *Abul-Banat*.

"Potatoes," Ahmed answered.

"So, you planted a girl, how do you expect to get a son?" he asked, with a twinkle in his eye. Ahmed quickly took his baby daughter and wife and returned to his village.

A rabbi was assigned to the hospital, and he often sat at the bedside of a dying patient all through the night, recited prayers, and presided over the religious washing and purifying rites of the deceased, and he did his best to comfort and offer solace to the bereaved. He also celebrat-

ed the religious services on holy days in our outpatients'
reception hall, which was furnished appropriately for every
special purpose. Any patient belonging to a non-Jewish faith
could also call his sheikh, minister or priest whenever he
wished to have him visit. The Brith-Milah (circumcision)
hall was situated in the gynecology ward. It contained as a
center piece, a wonderfully carved Brith-Milah chair that
had been presented as a gift by Baron Felix de Menashe.
Every Brith-Milah was a happening not only for the family
concerned, but for the entire hospital staff as well. Whoever
could find the necessary spare time to attend the ceremony
took part. All the participants were presented with a small,
artistic porcelain box filled with delicious almond sweets
called *drages*. I kept them as precious souvenirs of the events.

Wedding ceremonies usually took place at the grand
synagogue; and there too each of the guests attending the
wedding was presented with one of these beautiful ornate
containers full of delicious almond sweets. On the back of
these plates or boxes the names of the bride and the bridegroom were artistically carved, as well as the date of the
wedding celebration. Thus, they became beautiful souvenirs
of memorable wedding days. King Farouk himself was
sometimes invited, and he attended many Jewish wedding
ceremonies. He also sometimes attended morning services
at the grand synagogue, the "Gates of Heaven" in Cairo, or
in Alexandria on feasts and on Yom Kippur, because it was a
government-recognized holy day. Most of the schools, shops,
and businesses in the whole of Egypt were closed then, as
well as the government offices.

I learned to understand, admire, emulate and respect the mentality of the different ethnic groups, their various cultures, their warm responsibility toward their kin, and their close family ties. This was typical of both the Egyptian Jews and the Gentiles. Alexandria then, was a cosmopolitan center in the best sense of the word, and the Jewish hospital was in many ways a microcosm of this rich mosaic of a multi-cultural world, which functioned as a harmonious symphony. Many of the patients came back from time to time to thank us for our good services, and it always made me happy to see them again.

Most of the maintenance staff and orderlies came from the same family clan in the Sudan, by the name of Khalil. They were admirable in many ways. They were docile, friendly, and felt responsible for each other and helped one another whenever they could. Most of the women working in the laundry were Egyptian Moslems, and their manager, Aisha, a Moslem, too, who was respected and loved by all. I can't remember any theft from servants, patients, or staff in the hospital during the whole of my stay there. Honesty, devotion and dedication were everybody's key values. Some of our workers got special nicknames, and they were proud of them, as for example, "Aisha Pasha" in charge of the laundry, and "Abdel-Rahman Bey" the *boab* (gatekeeper); and "Regina Maria," the head cook who reigned supreme in her kitchen. Her staff included mostly Arabs, though Maria herself was Italian. She had a beautiful daughter, named Bella, whom she dearly cherished, and woe to us if we forgot to ask her for news about her daughter! I don't remember ever having seen her out of the kitchen. She was always there from early morning until late afternoons, and she loved being there, wearing a spotless white bonnet, presiding over her delicious cooking, tasting it over and over again, and breathing in the wonderful odors.

We had up-to-date surgical wards, as well as several modern and fully equipped internal wards; a large, very well-equipped laboratory, in which intensive research was conducted; a large pharmacy; a modern X-Ray Institute; and a polyclinic for outpatients. The hospital had third, second, and first-class rooms, but all the patients got the same minute care and attention.

The Hospital was cosmopolitan indeed, and a model of harmonious relations among people who came from various backgrounds. The head surgeon, Dr. Fritz Katz, the head physician, his first assistant, and the head of the laboratory were German Jews and they had Egyptian, Jewish and Moslem assistants. The head of the X-Ray Institute was a Greek from Rhodes who had studied in Germany, while his assistants were Egyptian Jews who had studied in England, France and Italy. The head gynecologist, as I mentioned before, was also an Egyptian Jew, as well as all his expert assistants. The midwife's aide was an Egyptian. Most of the staff began their work at the hospital between 1933 and 1935 and stayed to the end. The administrative offices were run by Egyptian Jews, and all the salaries and the funding of the hospital came from the Jewish community of Alexandria. The larger Jewish Hospital in Cairo which was built on a similar model, was funded by the Cairo Jewish Community.

The head of the Department of Internal Medicine was Professor Mainzer, who was previously attached to the University of Rostock, in Germany. Before coming to Alexandria, he had already made some remarkable research concerning *bilharzia*, a widely spread endemic disease among the poorer population. He continued his research at the hospital laboratory, with revolutionary results in the field. Many patients suffering from bilharzia came to the Hospital be treated by him, not only from Egypt but also from the neighboring countries, with excellent results. His scientific work made an impact in the field.

The prevalent serious diseases we treated at the hospital then were mostly typhoid fever, typhus (contracted from hair lice or clothes lice), malaria, diabetes, diphtheria, yellow fever, trachoma, bilharzia, and even some cholera cases, though we were not supposed to take them in. All infectious diseases had to be sent to the

Government Hospital, the "*Afna*," for treatment; but many people were afraid to go there and preferred to die at home in their own beds. It was said that whoever entered the "Afna" got out of it only as a corpse. Unfortunately, this sorrowful fact was often true.

Dr. Arbib, who was in charge of blood transfusions in our hospital, presented me with a revolutionary project-- the building of a blood bank. This was a very innovative and unusual enterprise for the times, and a forerunner of modern blood banks. I immediately realized its great potentialities, but it took all of the power of my rhetoric to convince the Board to approve the project. I explained to them that because of the hot climate, we were confronted by the necessity to have a constant supply of tested and labelled blood kept on ice. The idea for the blood bank was finally approved and it saved many lives. It also greatly helped us during the battle of El Alamein, when Rommel's Nazi army was just half an hour away from Alexandria. Many of the wounded Allied Forces' soldiers from the U.S., Australia, Canada, France, England, South Africa, and the Jewish Brigade from Palestine--were treated at our hospital where we worked very hard day and night to save their lives. It saved our lives too, for many of these recovered brave soldiers returned to the front, and they helped to win the battle against Rommel. After his defeat, they found that Rommel and his staff had long lists of every Jewish inhabitant in Egypt and minute orders to exterminate all of them.

The medical staff did its utmost in order to keep up-to-date with scientific progress in various medical fields. Medical scientists from all over the world visited our hospital, and they were impressed by the research and the effective and innovative blood bank which saved so many lives.

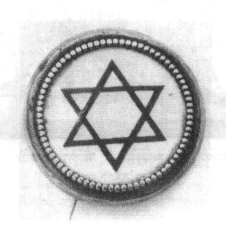

Thea's Nurse Pin

The Jewish Hospital in Alexandria

The Jewish Hospital staff in Alexandria.
Thea is in the middle of the second row,
behind Dr. Katz, the Head Surgeon

6

FOUR WIVES

One of our doctors, Dr. Karara, who was an Egyptian Moslem surgeon, had studied medicine in Germany and married a beautiful blonde German woman there. He became one of our assistants in our Surgical Department. His newly-wed wife, Gretchen, was terribly disappointed when she found out to her great dismay, on arriving at Alexandria, that she was Dr. Karara's wife number four! His three other wives were all alive and well, living together with their numerous children in a large house over which he duly reigned as a self-crowned sultan. According to the Muslim law, a man is allowed to have four wives, so she couldn't even sue him for bigamy. We tried our best to console her, but she could not overcome the shock and she wanted to divorce him and return immediately to Germany.

"Why didn't he tell me that in Germany?" she wailed, heartbroken. "I would have never married him if I knew!"

He begged her to stay, and at length she agreed, but on one condition, that he should leave Alexandria with her and go to work somewhere else, far from his other three wives.

Dr. Karara who loved Gretchen very much, eventually accepted, and became after some time, with our help, the chief surgeon of the Government Hospital in Rosette, in the delta of the Nile region. We assured him before taking over his new job that we would always help him and that whenever he was in need of anything he could turn to us. He did in fact, apply to us eventually with a very strange request.

"Everything is okay in Rosette," he assured me one day, smiling his enchanting Egyptian warm smile under his profuse mustache. Later, I realized how much he resembled the actor Omar Sharif, with his dewy eyes and all. "But could you do me a great favor, please?"

"Oh, for sure," I answered readily. "What is it you want me to do for you?"

"You see, "he said hesitatingly, "I don't get a fixed salary and am being paid according to the number of operations I perform, such as appendectomies or hernia operations. Could I ask you to preserve some appendices and hernia skins for me please from the operations you perform at the Jewish Hospital?"

I was stupefied by this strange request. "But what will you do with them?" I asked in surprise.

"I can then send them on to the Government Health Department and therefore receive a reasonable salary, as the number of hernia skins and appendices is counted there and I am paid accordingly," he explained apologetically. I thought of the four wives he had to take care of, as well as his many children and smiled understandingly.

I consulted Dr. Katz about this bizarre request, and he immediately agreed to help Dr. Karara. "Four wives is not an easy task." he said ruefully. "I haven't decided yet to wed even one, myself," he added with a bright twinkle in his eye. I knew he had from time to time, romantic adventures with voluptuous ladies, and was glad he never made any advances to me. He always kept the promise he had made to my parents and treated me like his own close sister. Dr. Karara came to the hospital from time to time to collect his precious appendices and hernia skins which we kept on ice, and was very grateful to us for our help.

Unfortunately, the poor surgeon did not last long. He got diphtheria from one of his patients and passed away when still quite young, leaving his four bereaved wives and numerous children behind. Gretchen consoled herself at length, and returned to Germany after the end of World War Two. "You know, I would have never believed it," she confided in me, "but he was so loving and charming that in time, I forgot I was number four, and now that he's dead I miss him so!"

***

Speaking of Rosette, I now remember my first visit to the region, where I was sent to treat some trachoma cases with a new drug we developed at the hospital. The simple *fellahin* farmers were very grateful, hospitable and kind to us. I admired their dignity and self-composure, their warmth of heart, and their instinctive sensibility and delicacy of nature, despite their great poverty.

"What have you learned, Sister Thea, on your first day in an Egyptian village?" Dr. Katz asked me curiously on my return.

"These friendly folk, who can neither read nor write," I responded pensively, "are sometimes far wiser and more patient than I and many educated people I know, who have trained themselves all their lives to attain the fruits of culture and of knowledge. They seem to have an instinctive culture and affective tendency all of their own," I added, "as well as a special sense of humor and knack to laugh at themselves and at their drawbacks--which was quite an experience for me. I don't know where it stems from, but it's surely admirable..."

Dr. Katz nodded his approval, "perhaps from their ancient Pharaonic culture," he added whimsically.

"Well, I hope one day they will all be as well-off as it seems they were in Pharaonic times," I remarked. "Their poverty and lack of minimal standards of living were so blatant, that I pitied them with all my heart."

Thea in the Hospital Garden (1940)

Celebrating Rosh Hashana at the Jewish Hospital (1934)

7

MICROCOSM

As I mentioned before, the families of all of our employees were treated at the hospital free of charge. We also performed circumcisions on the sons of our Moslem employees when they had reached the age of thirteen, which of course was a more serious operation than when they were babies, as with the Jews. But they never brought the girls for clitorectomy, which was still very much in vogue then. They knew that we considered it an amputation for which there was no biological or moral reason whatever, and that we would not accept doing it. Unfortunately, I hear it is still a custom in some parts of Egypt and other Islamic countries to this day. I recently read a moving book, *The Hidden Face of Eve*, by Nawal El Sartawi, a doctor who had herself been a victim of a cruel clitorectomy at the age of six, and dedicated part of her life to protest against this operation which rendered girls sexual invalids for life. She was later put in prison for

having written such a revolutionary book against a traditional Moslem custom. I wished then, and wish to this day, that
this barbarous tradition would soon be abolished and that
it would free women from so much unnecessary pain and
misery.

None of our staff--neither nurses, helpers, nor clean-
ers--accepted money as an expression of thanks for the good
service the patient was given. The concept of 'baksheesh,'
tipping, was strange to us and against all that the hospital
stood for. All the staff and patients understood that, and they
respected the spirit and the unwritten law of the hospital. It
was known to everybody who came to be treated that nobody
accepted money. If one wanted to donate some money for the
staff, it was given for this purpose to the employee in charge
of the administrative office. The sum was then distributed
among the entire staff on an equal basis, approximately every
two or three months. Thus, there was no danger of bribery or
preferential status.

We had a storeroom for clothes, shoes, and underwear
for those patients who were in need of clothing when they
left the hospital. They very often also received the necessary
money for either a taxi to take them home or for the bus
fare. In our large Outpatient Department, the patients were
examined, treated, and given the prescribed medicine all for
a minimum sum. When the patients were poor or needy, it
was entirely free. Later, this clothes storeroom served us to
cater for the thousands of refugees who fled the Nazi regime
from all over Europe and Africa: Germany, Czechoslovakia,
France, Hungary, Romania, Greece, Libya and Tunisia.

The hospital was not only a center for healing and restoring physical health, it was also a kind of institution where everybody who came for help received it. It became, in time, a center for psychological consultation and advice for worries or problems of any sort. That is, it catered not only to the body but also to the psyche. This was one of our greatest achievements and we were all proud of it. People came to us for advice on family, educational, marital and sex problems as well as psychological problems, and were taken care of by well-trained, responsible and devoted doctors and nurses. Thus, we developed our own social-work system, which greatly helped us when the multitude of fugitives from the Nazi regime frenziedly knocked at our doors almost every single day.

When World War Two broke out, both Mr. and Mrs. Nahman who were diligent and hard-working volunteers at the Hospital, organized a Volunteer Committee which was comprised of many women and men, not only from the Jewish community but also Moslems, Christians, Copts, and from other ethnic groups in Alexandria, most of them Egyptian citizens, who donated their time at the disposal of the hospital. Both Mr. and Mrs. Nahman were very active at the hospital and volunteered most of their time to it. Mr. Raphael Nahman, who was a retired architect, served as a member of the Board of Directors of the Hospital; he was in charge of buying the equipment. Mrs. Eliane Nahman, his wife, was a benevolent volunteer at the Hospital, who did her best to daily comfort the chronically sick patients. During the Second World War, she also became the Deputy Chief of the ARP--*Air Raid Passive Defense Force*. Mrs. Ades, also a Jewish woman, was the chief of this exemplary organization. Among the volunteers were, Princess Amina Toussoun, a close relative of King Farouk's; Fawzeya, the wife of the mayor of Alexandria; and also, many other women whose husbands were high officials. They all worked tirelessly on a purely volunteer basis; they never complained or abandoned their posts. They came daily on duty like all the staff and gave a helping hand wherever they were needed in all the different wards and departments of the hospital. Many of them even continued to help us after the end of the war, because they had become so attached to the hospital and patients, and to each of us personally.

Everyone who wanted to be treated at the hospital was admitted. Very often it was a poor Arab *fellah* (farmer) who couldn't afford the hospital fees. There was no government health insurance in Egypt then, and the poor suffered. Neither was there any private medical insurance to speak of except for *La Mutuelle des Employes,* therefore, the patient himself usually had to pay for his hospitalization and the treatment. Exceptions were made for those patients who were under the care of the Jewish community and were considered to be welfare cases, and for the needy in general. Our doors were open day and night. The servants were very honest people and worked as hard as we did, often for ten hours a day. They got one day off a week, and one-week yearly vacation. They were cheerful and good-humored, and I can't remember any of them being absent. They had their meals at the hospital; they were orderly, disciplined, clean, and entirely devoted.

At the official opening of the hospital, in June 1932, King Fouad himself, the father of Farouk, attended the opening ceremony, as well as several high government officials. In time, the good reputation and high medical standard of the hospital spread not only in Egypt, but also in the entire Middle East and the whole world. We were proud of that and felt rewarded for our efforts.

One of our greatest achievements was the warm atmosphere of a big family firmly united by a common goal. We tried to do our utmost in order to heal and nurse all our patients equally, no matter what their status, creed or nationality was. We had patients from almost everywhere, including France, England, America, Italy, Syria, Lebanon, Sudan, Greece, Cyprus, Rhodes, and Persia. When during World War Two Malta was bombed by the German Luftwaffe, we also treated wounded civilians brought from Malta by the Royal British Air Force. They were usually sinewy, strong and the color of light, copper sunshine. I felt great pity to see such strength and vigor disabled by my enemy, war, and hated it more than ever.

Thus, the hospital was indeed a microcosm of the world, containing staff and patients of all citizenships and beliefs; and we all worked together harmoniously to attain our humane goal of healing and saving lives. This is what I hoped the world would be one day, no ethnic or religious barriers, all working together for the good of humanity. I was delighted by the challenge, but also overwhelmed by the responsibility. During the first year I felt as if I was carrying the whole world on my frail shoulders, but in time they strengthened, and the tremendous work gave me great satisfaction and a fulfilling sense of creativeness. "I am needed and useful, I am saving human beings, my life is not in vain!" my heart sang in me. The same feelings were shared by every person working at the hospital. As I felt confident and fulfilled inside my skin, I had the ability to make other people feel comfortable, useful and important. This could be clearly detected on their usually cheerful faces, and it made mine doubly radiant.

Physicians, Nurses and Servants of the Surgery Department and Gynecology Department at the Hospital Thea stands in the middle.

8

MOTHER OF PEACE

I remember an incident which occurred in the spring of 1933 during my second year of work at the hospital. It often happened that the chief surgeon, Dr. Katz, was called to do some minor surgery at the palace of the well-known Pasha Amir. We usually took Massoud, our helper in the Surgical Department, with us to prepare a small operating room at the palace, in which Dr. Katz carried out the surgery. Often, I had to stay with the patient for a few days after, in order to take care of him. Once we had to operate on Pasha Amir for a badly broken ankle, which happened while he was riding his horse in his gorgeous palace grounds. On that occasion, I had to nurse him for three weeks.

Penicillin was then available only as a powder, and it had to be prepared for every injection. One day there was a short circuit in the main part of the palace, and I had to go to the kitchen, which was situated on the ground floor, in order to sterilize the syringe. Pasha Amir, with his straight, streaked gray hair, his high cheekbones, old gold skin, and almond eyes, looked more like a Pharaonic King than a Moslem Pasha. He warned me that Mohammed, the head cook, was a very hot-tempered man, and that they had been on bad terms for some time. I went down to the neat and clean kitchen adorned with expensive blue and white china on hazel nut shelves. I introduced myself to Mohammed and asked him politely for permission to sterilize the syringes for the pasha. The tall black haired and black-eyed Mohammed, who was also the economist in charge of the storerooms, was civil, and he kindly put everything I needed, including the gas oven, at my disposal. As I had to stay there for about twenty minutes until the injection was sterilized, I started talking to him.

"I congratulate you for the wonderful meals you prepare for the Pasha and for me," I said, "and for his many friends who come to pay him their respects." I paused, then added, "The pasha is very grateful for your kind services."

The cook looked at me in disbelief, and an angry look appeared in his eyes. I saw his muscles tensing but he didn't say a word.

"Why don't you come up one of these days and bring the meals to the pasha yourself and wish him a quick recovery?" I suggested.

"Why? Isn't he angry with me anymore?" he inquired in a surprised tone

"No," I said, "he isn't angry at all. So why don't you come with me and say *salaam aleikum* to him? It will do him good, and both of you can make up and live in peace."

"*Tayeb, ya set.* Okay, Miss," he said, rather reluctantly. He prepared a beautiful meal consisting of a delicious '*moloheya*,' a green spinach like soup, baked chicken and potatoes, raisin and almond rice, and a *basboussa* cake as dessert, on a silver tray, and we both went up to the pasha's room. Then Mohammed suddenly tautly stopped at the door and looked blank, not daring to enter.

The pasha at first was a bit confused. He looked at the cook and at me, and then said, "Come in please, Mohammed. I want to thank you for the good meals you always prepare for me. Come in!"

Mohammed went in, kissed the hand of his employer, turned to me, and said, "*Ya sister, hoa ragel kwais, awi, awi, awi.* "Sister, he is a very, very, very good man." Then he quickly left the room in confusion.

From then on Mohammed himself brought the meals to the pasha's room. He was proud that after working twenty years as a cook, the pasha finally raised his salary, congratulating him for his excellent meals and for keeping meticulous accounts. Weeks later Mohammed came to pay me a visit at the hospital and brought me a basket with various kinds of fruit, butter and eggs from his own small cottage. "Everything is all right, *sistte*," he said joyfully. "It is Allah himself who sent you to my kitchen, as an *Om el Salaam*[2] in order to make peace between my master and me."

I smiled happily, marveling at the fact how the right words in the right place can sometimes do wonders. "Thank

---

2   *Om el salaam*: mother of peace, in Arabic.

you very much, Mohammed, for all the good things you have brought us," I said. "And if in case, God forbid, you or somebody of your family becomes sick or needs our help, you will always be welcome at the hospital and will be treated like part of my own family. Now I'll go and bring this lovely fruit basket to the kitchen so that everybody can taste it."

"But the fruit basket is for you, Sister Thea, not for everybody," he protested.

"Sharing things with people makes me much happier, Mohammed, than tasting fruit by myself," I explained gently to him

"*Allah yekhaliki!*" "God bless you!" he replied, and smiled gratefully, that typical spontaneous genuine Egyptian smile which is so difficult to match and which never failed to warm my heart.

That episode has stayed with me for more than half a century, and when a story remains fresh in my mind after such a long time, it almost always contains a lesson which will benefit me, and perhaps other people as well. The key lies in what is today called 'conflict resolution,' trying to find the common ground in a conflicting situation, so as to bridge the differences in a harmonious and constructive way. I realize today, that living on good terms with one's neighbors and *entourage* is an art and a technique which can be taught, learned and developed. Of course, one will need the basic values and tools to build upon; they are the love of life and of human beings; the ability to change oneself from a crawling creature bent down by rancor to a convivial one with open wings flying freely, high in the skies.

Most of all, we need to remember that we are created creative and can invent new situations, rules and new relationships, as frequently as they are needed, so as to live more constructive and harmonious lives. Frustration, anger, hatred, and the feeling of helplessness that we are unable to change a given situation, can imprison and inhibit more finally than iron chains and barred windows. An important quotation from Virginia Woolf in Three Guineas, comes back to my mind, *"We cannot use your words and your methods, but have to create new words and new methods...."*

Letterhead of the Jewish Hospital in Alexandria

9

THE TURKISH PRINCE

I got to know and to admire the spiritual qualities of many of our patients. One of those I will always remember is Nina Mosseri, a venerated member of one of the well-known *Sephardi* (Spanish) Jewish families in town. She arrived at the hospital in January 1934, with a serious kidney condition. Yet she always smiled her seemingly two-thousand-year-old smile, which I learned to know and appreciate. Whenever I had the time in the evenings I brought her meals in myself, and sat down next to her for a chat. It always brightened up her wise, ancient, freckled face.

"It's quite normal, I told my granddaughter yesterday," Nina remarked, "that she should rebel against her father's values, as he did against his father's and I against both my father and mother. What a daredevil I was in those days! Thea, did I tell you the story of how I got married to Victor, my husband? May he rest in peace."

"No, Nina, I don't think so," I answered. I always enjoyed hearing her stories. It was a quiet evening in the ward, and I had completed all my duties, so I sat comfortably in the armchair by her side, with a bowl of beautiful red roses between us.

"As you perhaps know already," she started, "my father was the director of the National Bank of Egypt in Port Said. All this goes back to the beginning of the century, as you understand. We lived then on the second floor of a nice, comfortable house, just over the bank. One day when I was seventeen years old, one of my father's most prominent clients, a Turkish prince by the name of Fawzi Emir, saw me and fell in love with me. It was a tragedy! He asked father for my hand, and we all got the shock of our lives. Father was astounded. He knew what it meant to refuse such a proposal in Ottoman-ruled Egypt. The Emir could easily have him beheaded, and I would have been taken away by force to his harem. Father tactfully tried to remind the prince that I was Jewish, but the prince answered that it didn't matter, as when he was deeply in love, he usually overlooked such petty details.

"'I assure you Mosseri Bey, that your lovely daughter will be looked after as well as any of my Moslem wives,' he told my father.

"Father didn't lose his wits; he made excuses to the prince that I was already betrothed to his head clerk and that the wedding was to take place a month later. The head clerk, Mr. Jacobs, had indeed asked for my hand, but both Father and I had refused him. For one thing, he was eighteen years older than I, bald and fat and in addition, a widower with two kids! But having said that to the prince, there was no way out. Father set out immediately to arrange the wedding, declaring, 'Better a bald Jew, than a Turkish harem!'

"I wept and cried, 'But I don't love Jacobs!'

"'So what? Do you prefer the Turkish prince?' my father asked.

"'You'll love him after the wedding my dear, you'll see,' my helpless mother tried to console me. 'Jacobs is a kind-hearted and intelligent man; I'm sure he'll find the way to your heart in time.'

"'But he's old, heavy and ugly, and I don't love him!' I cried in exasperation, tears flowing down my cheeks.

"'What's love before marriage, you silly girl, my father cried. 'It doesn't exist.'

"'I won't marry him, I won't, I won't, I won't!' I shouted frantically, when the time came closer.

"'You'll do exactly as you're told, my girl, my father said severely, 'or the Turkish prince will take you to his harem and have us all persecuted.'

"'There's no such thing as love before marriage,' my mother pleaded tearfully again.

"But in my heart, I knew that love existed before marriage, because the summer before, when we were visiting our Aunt Claire in Cairo, I met my handsome, red-haired, second cousin Victor again, and we fell deeply in love. We mostly communicated with our eyes, as there was nowhere safe to meet far from our parents' frowns. We kept it a secret, because we knew my father would never approve of such a match. For

THE WOMAN IN WHITE | 97

one thing, we were second cousins; secondly, Victor was only one year older than I was; he had just finished school and had not yet started to work. His father, moreover, did not have any position to speak of, as he was a simple clerk at one of the Jewish stores in town.

"When I saw that my father was adamant and that the preparations for the wedding with Jacob were under way, I had no other choice. I fled to Victor in Cairo, and tearfully told him the whole story. Victor was shocked and wanted to marry me straightaway, but his parents wouldn't hear of it, and they insisted on sending me back to Port Said.

'There's no way out,' Victor said. 'We have to take our fate into our own hands.'

"He wiped my tears and looking at me with his big beautiful hazel eyes--much the same color as yours, Thea, and he said, 'Now that you have come to me, Nina, I won't ever let you go!' He became my knight in armor who was going to save me from the Turkish dragon.

"We fled to Alexandria, where we eloped. On the next day, we were wed by an old, retired rabbi who believed, or pretended to believe our story that we were both orphans from Cairo and had no relatives to help us get married. He chuckled secretly throughout the ceremony and lent us his own ring when he found out we didn't have any. I think he secretly guessed we had eloped, and thoroughly enjoyed the part he was playing.

"When my father heard what had happened, he was furious. He swore I wasn't his daughter anymore, that he would never admit me into his house, and we wouldn't ever have a penny from him. Seeing how miserable and betrayed father felt, the Turkish prince eventually forgave him, judging that it was enough punishment for him to have lost a daughter to a penniless schoolboy in Cairo.

"We tried to manage on our own, Victor and I, but from time to time mother sent me a little money in secret, without my father's knowledge. Victor who found work in a shop, earned very little and I went to look for work. As you can imagine, in those days a Jewish woman from the middle-class who worked out of the house was something unheard of. But I didn't care; I loved Victor and wanted to be with him, close to his smiling freckled face and his flaming red hair...." A nostalgic half-smile appeared on Nina's trembling lips, and her eyes became distant and misty. She was again beautiful then, despite her deep wrinkles, and I could well imagine how young Victor fell in love with her.

Nina continued, "I finally took a short nursing course, and got a job as a private nurse. For years I nursed the Princess Zulfikar, who later introduced me to the nobility, and in time, to the royal family, too. I nursed them all, young and old, from the blooming of the fragrant jasmine in spring to the rising of the Nile in winter.

"We knew there was no other way out--I had to work, and I learned a great deal from those years. I learned how to stand on my own two feet, and yet to be a supporting and loving partner to my dear Victor. Five years later, when we had saved enough, Victor opened a textile business in the Khamzawi, in the heart of the *Mouski*, and I could stay at home part of the time, to raise my three fine children. We never gave up; that's the secret, *ya binti* (my daughter), and I know you're of the same stuff, Thea; I've been watching you closely, you never give up either. This, Schwester Thea, we have in common. And to this day," her eyes became misty again, and she put her palm over her frail breast, "I have Victor's red flaming hair and his sweet, tender smile in my heart, warming me on cold, damp days, when this bothersome kidney aches more than ever." She sighed nostalgically, and had the faraway, peaceful look which people who have had a full life are blessed with. I bent over Nina and kissed her; I always felt close to her, even when we had arguments about her injections and she vehemently protested that we gave her far too many, and that this should definitely be the last one, as it would kill her anyway.

A special quality I admired in Nina was that she seemed to me to be in some strange way ahead of her time. She had somehow managed to escape the claws of the limited, traditional feminine role of her day. Having started to work as a nurse at such an early stage must have developed in her faculties which were uncommon to women then, even in the West. Now, after hearing the story of Victor, I understood how the circumstances of her life had helped her to attain progressive views.

"This is why I later joined the Society for the Liberation of Women during Saad Zaghloul's time," she explained, uncannily reading my thoughts.

"A woman's liberation movement in the beginning of the century, and in Egypt?" I cried in astonishment.

"When I first joined, I was amazed," Nina continued. "I

had never seen so many women together before. The large parlor we met in was sometimes so full, that some of the younger women had to sit on cushions or on the carpet. The meetings were animated, and I could feel that the women were enthusiastic and very involved. I'll never forget our leader Hakima. She was a beautiful, well-dressed young woman with large black eyes and smooth, jet-black flowing hair, which shone brightly as she spoke. She conducted the meetings smoothly and fired us with her enthusiasm and staunch beliefs. She firmly maintained, for instance, that women had the right to vote, and to file divorces.[3] The talks were always followed by lively discussions, all in Arabic of course. I was fascinated and influenced by the spirit of those women's ideology then, and it built a firm cornerstone in my heart, for me, my daughters, and my granddaughters, who all hold democratic views as to the equal rights of men and women.

"Do you feel then that women should have the same opportunities as men?" I asked her quizzically, knowing in my heart what her answer would be, and loving her for it.

"What a question! Aren't we of the same flesh and blood?" Her eyes flashed brightly. "We do not live in a democratic society yet, but we will get there. One day we shall have exactly the same opportunities as men and the same

---

3   According to Islamic law, it is enough for a husband to tell his wife, before a witness, "woman you are divorced," four times for the divorce to be legal. Furthermore, only a man has the right to divorce his wife, and not the other way around. This law is still enforced today.

rights before the law. We're just as intelligent as they are!" She paused and waved her delicate veined hand in my direction, "And you're a fine example, Thea!"

I laughed and kissed her good night, and shut the door softly behind me. When she passed away a month later, I felt as if a member of my own family had disappeared. Nina had a full and creative life, I tried to console myself. She had principles and lived by them. She did not live in vain.

10

THE CERTIFICATE

Another of our outstanding women patients was Flora Matalon, who came to the hospital in the autumn of 1935 with jaundice and a bad liver condition. When she eventually recovered, she told me a delightful story which happened in her youth.

"Which school are you in, Mademoiselle?" the French inspector sent to orally examine the pupils for the certificate diploma, asked Flora Matalon, impressed by her knowledge of French and literature.

"The Jewish School, Monsieur, *l'ecole de la Communaute Juive*, thirteen-year-old Flora said. On that day, the school yard was full of thirteen-year-old youngsters who had come to be examined for the prestigious French Government Certificate, from various schools in Alexandria and the neighboring towns.

"*Parlez nous de la Palestine, Mademoiselle,*" "Tell us

a little about Palestine, Miss," the French inspector told her somewhat sarcastically, "as you come from the Jewish school." Palestine was not in the program, but Flora in 1916 was already a Zionist at heart, as her father and grandfather before her, who had taught her to love *"Haaretz"* Israel, the land of her forefathers.

She did not hesitate and started relating what she knew. She spoke with such enthusiasm that a brilliant light shone from her beautiful, honey-colored eyes. She explained the traditional Jewish prayer and wish at Passover: "Next year in Jerusalem," excitedly. It seemed as if part of her soul gushed out with the current of her words: words of love, of longing, and a two-thousand-years aspiration for the return to the Promised Land--Zion.

"This is what Zionist means," she ended breathlessly, "it means the love of Zion, and the wish to return to the Land of Zion, or the Land of Israel, which are both the same."

The Gentile inspector realizing that the young girl standing proudly before him was not only a Jew, but also a Zionist, asked coldly, "Have you ever been to Palestine?"

"*Non, Monsieur.*"

"If you love Zion the land of your forefathers so much, without even having seen it, perhaps you should draw it for us on the board," he said, half-amused, half-ironic.

Flora hesitated for one instant only. It flashed through her mind that he was taunting her; he thought she would not know how to draw the map of Palestine. But she did. She took the piece of chalk in her hesitating fingers and with quick strokes, she drew the Palestine of her day on the shiny blackboard, marking Haifa, Tel Aviv, and Jerusalem, the Dead Sea, and the Sea of Galilee. Then with dotted lines she indicated what used to be "Israel," the Land of the Bible, as her grandfather had lovingly taught her.

Before she finished, she turned around and glanced timidly at the inspector. Her heart fell. The man's leering smile had disappeared; he stood upright and tense, with a stern and forbidding expression on his face, as if he had caught her stealing or breaking some of the ten commandments. Even his moustache seemed bristling in anger. She realized that if she continued the biblical map, she might fail her examination and a cold shiver ran down her spine. That would mean that she wouldn't be admitted to the coveted *Lycee* High School, and the dashing of all her dreams for a brilliant future career, as her parents had planned for her.

"Should I pretend I forgot how to continue?" she asked herself with sinking heart. "But that would be a lie."

She hated lying. "Be true first of all to yourself," her grandfather's words came back to her. She felt as though waves rolled inside her in all directions and they became a full, rich cascade of clear, transparent meaning.

Her fingers stopped shaking as she gripped the chalk firmly, faced the half-blank blackboard, and filled it with lines, tracing the full map of Palestine as she knew it then.

"Thank you, Mademoiselle," the Inspector said curtly, "you may leave now," he added dismissing her with an impatient wave of his hand, as he would do to a troublesome fly.

"I failed the examination, I won't have my certificate

now," she thought sadly, "but at least I was true to myself," she consoled herself on leaving the classroom. The inspector watched her silently, but the deep wrinkles around his mouth seemed to accuse her this time of having broken *all* of the ten commandments at once.

A month later the answer arrived from the French Government. Surprisingly, she had passed the examination with flying colors! Her golden-lettered diploma soon arrived from France, and her father had it framed and hung it up proudly in the drawing room near the blue box of the *Keren Kayemet* - the Fund for the Land of Israel. Flora was admitted to the *Lycee* and later had a brilliant career as a teacher of French Literature and Philosophy.

"Despite the fact, and perhaps because of the fact," she said smiling, "that I remained true to myself." The stars in her brown velvety eyes shown brighter than ever. I patted her hand tenderly and thanked her for having shared her moving and significant story with me.

Flora left the hospital a week later. We all missed her; she had become such a familiar and beloved face in our hospital. In 1956, she left Egypt for *Haaretz*, the land of Israel that she loved. She lives there today in *Kiryat Ata*, with her children, who have children of their own. Each of them lives on one of the dots their mother Flora had courageously drawn on the Alexandrian blackboard more than three quarters of a century ago: Jerusalem, Tel Aviv and Haifa.

The school mentioned above was the sister School of the Jewish Community in Abasseya, in Cairo, which had once been proudly owned by *l'Alliance Juive Universelle*.

106 | ADA AHARONI

The sponsors of both of these prestigious schools were two prominent Jewish Egyptian leaders: Mr. Jacques Mosseri and Mr. Katawi Pasha. Both families were bankers, and they owned the Mosseri Bank and the Katawi Bank respectively. They tried to get the best teachers with the highest standards for both schools, where French, English, Hebrew and Arabic were taught. In each of these two Jewish Community schools there were approximately four hundred boys and four hundred girls in 1916, from the ages of six to eighteen. The wise, learned, and dedicated directors were Mr. Jacob Caleff, and Mr. Moise Sherezeli and his wife Claire, who lovingly catered for both the minds and the hearts of their pupils.

"Every time the Headmaster pronounced the word *"Haaretz"* (Land of Israel), Flora said wistfully, "my heart would beat fast with yearning for our promised land, as if it would break. We were all taught the language of our forefathers," she reported, her eyes shining as two bright torches, "both boys and girls. And we sang in Hebrew with all our lungs and hearts, until Israel just had to happen, and exist again!" She caught her breath and continued, "When Haim Weizman, who later became the first President of the State of Israel, came to visit our school, he was so surprised and pleased when we sang in Hebrew, that when I handed him the flowers we had prepared for him, he even kissed me on the cheek!" Flora said blushing, as if she was thirteen again.

11

NIGHT OF THE STAIRCASE

One warm evening, in the spring of 1936, when I was on night duty, I sat by the bedside of a pretty, but somewhat sad-looking young Jewish-Egyptian mother, by the name of Emily. She had given birth to a fine baby girl three days before, and therefore her sorrowful looks intrigued me.

"Why are you so sad, Emily?" I asked her. "You seem to have a charming husband, and now you have a beautiful and healthy baby. So why the mournful face?"

Emily looked at me with her bright brown eyes. "It all began on the night of the staircase," she murmured sadly. "Would you like to hear the story, Sister Thea?"

"Oh, yes!" I nodded enthusiastically. These stories I heard from my patients gave me a deeper insight into what growing up in Egypt meant.

"Well, one afternoon, when I was seven years old," Emily began to relate, "my mother came to my room and said,

'We're going to Nona,[4] your grandmother Regina.'

"To my surprise, when we got there, Nona stood in the doorway, barring it with her big impressive body, and was firm in her refusal to let us in.

"'What's happening tonight?' I asked myself in bewilderment. Nona was usually so glad when we came to see her, and she always had such delicious cakes and chocolate for us.

"'Don't be silly. It doesn't pay to be *zaalana*. Go back to your husband, Rachel,' Nona chided my mother coaxingly. 'Most husbands in Egypt are the same, they all end up by sleeping with these wanton girl servants. Is this a logical reason for you to leave him?'

"'I'll never go back, never, never!' my mother repeated in a voice as if the world had come to an end. I didn't know what the meaning of *zaalana* was, but I supposed it was something like *stupid,* and I was angry with my grandmother for calling my mother names.

"'It never pays to be *zaalana*,' Nona repeated firmly, still refusing to let the three of us in.

"Years later I learned that to be *zaalana* (angry and hurt) was a widespread social convention in Egypt. When a wife had been deeply hurt by her husband and felt she had to do something drastic, instead of throwing herself into the Nile, she used to pack herself and her children away to her mother's. A *zaalana* woman usually carried a *boga*, a round bundle comprising some clothing and belongings, as one takes camping. True to form, my mother and I were

---

4   *Nona* means grandmother in Ladino.

each carrying our *boga*. My two-year-old brother, Dodi, was too small to carry any, so my mother was carrying him in addition to her *boga*. My grandmother just saw the *bogas* and understood what had happened. Afraid that the 'camping' at her home might be too prolonged, she took a firm stand right from the beginning.

"'And what will you do with yourself and the children?' she continued. 'You know I can't support you, your father is out of work again, and what I earn as a private nurse is barely enough to live on and to go on keeping this house. Princess Fahida, my present patient is generous enough, but with those tuberculosis lung cases, there's no knowing how long she'll last. And what she pays me is not enough to feed three extra mouths. So be wise, and go back to your husband, Rachel, before it's too late, *mon chou-chou!*'

"She hurriedly kissed the three of us, pushed us away, and shut the door energetically behind us.

"My mother, still holding Dodi in her arms, sat on the doorstep and wept an ocean. My heart broke. I was all on my mother's side, without really knowing what it was all about. In my mind, mother was always right, especially when she cried. My father had done something to hurt her, and this something was linked with sleeping with our maid, Sayeda. I didn't see why it was such a terrible thing. When my mother had been away in Alexandria to visit my sick Aunt Becky; I had slept with Sayeda myself. Why my father wanted to sleep with the maid was another puzzle. He was big and strong and wasn't afraid of the dark shapes under the bed, like me. But nobody asked me, so I kept silent, faithful to the prevalent educational motto in Egypt that children should be seen and not heard.

"But mother's tears flooded my heart, and I cried with her, feeling waves of pity surging, and a deep frustration at my inability to help her.

"'I'll never go back to the house again!' she wept. 'But what will become of us? What in the world will become of us? Little Dodi woke up and quickly joined the crying choir; the three of us cried together in three different notes. My brother wailed the loudest, astonished that this time he had an unusual accompaniment, without of course having the faintest idea what it was all about. He was always ready for a good cry and had never had the opportunity before of having a general one in which his elders readily participated of their own free will. He therefore bawled out loudly to his heart's content, until he got tired, sucked his thumb, and fell asleep on my mother's heaving breast again.

"I was just seven years old then, but I still remember the dead, lost feeling, as if we were abandoned by the whole world. Nobody loves us, nobody wants us, my heart cried in pain. I wiped my mother's tears with my smudgy fingers, and they left two dark blotches like a delta on her cheeks, spreading all over her delicate face. I kissed her and tried to reassure her, 'I'm here, mamica, and will always be with you. And so, will Dodi,' I added.

"'Why didn't I learn a profession or trade?' mother sobbed. 'Why didn't he allow me to go on teaching my music lessons? Why did he have to sell my piano? I could have supported you if I had a job, and we wouldn't need him. If I could only work, if I could only be free!' She wept and sighed heartbreakingly.

"I hated my father then for selling my mother's piano. If I had money I would have bought her a fine large piano right on the spot; even in the middle of the night.

"'But why can't you work?' I asked.

"'Ca *ne se fait pas*'. It's not done. A Jewish woman of my standing cannot work. It's this stupid society of ours!' she sighed deeply as if she had lost all the hope in the world.

"I pondered what she said. If it was stupid, then why abide by it? Why did grown-ups like doing stupid things, sometimes?

"'Will Dodi work when he grows up?' I asked suddenly.

"'Of course, Dodi will work. He's not a girl, he's a boy! He will be a man,' she said proudly, holding my baby brother affectionately. I looked at the sleeping Dodi, sucking his thumb. It seemed so ridiculous that he, with his small hands and feet and such few teeth, Dodi, with his plump thumb in his tiny mouth, would work and be free to do whatever he wanted, and mother couldn't and neither could I, because she was a woman, and I was a girl. The injustice of it struck me like a slap across the face. I made a decision there and then that night on the stairs, the second major decision of my life, and perhaps one of the rare ones to which I have always been true: *I would work*. Whatever they say, 'done or not done,' I would never be dependent on anybody, or on any man, like my mother. I would be free, like Dodi.

"I kissed my mother reassuringly again on her beautiful chestnut hair and looked deeply into her honey eyes. 'It'll be all right, Mama,' I whispered. 'I will work. I won't be stupid. I will work like Dodi and bring home money. I'll buy you a big black shiny piano and you'll give music lessons again, and we'll both be free.' She smiled through her tears, but her smile contained a fountain of sadness. Patting me over the head she sighed and her sigh sounded like the wailing of the sea on the shores of Camp Caesar in Alexandria, on dark and stormy nights.

"I had made the first major decision of my life a year earlier, when I started school, at the age of six at the *Lycee*. Looking at the two pictures of 'Toto' in my first reading book, *Toto rit* and *Toto pleure*, I decided that the laughing Toto was so much nicer and jollier than the crying one, and that I wanted to be like him. I would always be a laughing Emily and not a crying one, I decided in my first week of school.

"But here I was on my grandmother's stairs crying! And so was my mother. It had seemed quite clear to me at the age of six, when I was in the first class, that a person's attitude was her own choice. You choose the rules you want to play in life, your actions, your values, your smiles, your tears, like activating the Guignol puppets I received on my birthday, and which I liked so much. My Guignol always laughed and smiled, he never wept, because I never made him cry. And here I was at seven, weeping on my grandmother's stairs, and so was my mother! And I couldn't stop my tears. What was clear to me at six, wasn't so clear to me anymore at seven.

"'*Je n'ai pas de la chance*,' my mother muttered, rocking little Dodi. 'I have no luck; I was born on a star-crossed night,' she wailed. My mother never agreed with me on the subject of free choice. She always had a blind faith in fate.

"'Don't worry mama,' I repeated soothingly, 'I promise you, I will always work and we will all be free.'

"That night I talked to my mother, there on my Nona's staircase, almost as if I were an adult; as if I could really help. I nodded my head and was angry at my father. There in the dark, flattered by my mother's confidence in me, I became almost a professional confidante, with an ear as big as my small fist. I tried to ask the right questions and answer the right replies, in a responsible way and a solemn voice. I became overnight, on that memorable *Night of the Staircase*, my mother's keeper. This feeling of deep responsibility toward my mother born on the *Night of the Staircase*, has accompanied me all my life.

"And now, at the age of twenty, and myself a mother, I ask myself again; perhaps my mother was right about the impossibility of free choice, and I was wrong," Emily ended bitterly. At this point I interrupted her.

"But what has all this to do with you today, why are you so unhappy now?"

Emily heaved a deep sigh and her fingers trembled slightly on the flowered bedcover. "David, my husband, doesn't want me to work anymore. He told me yesterday that I would never go back to the Travel Agency," she burst out, her bright brown eyes brimming with tears.

"Probably until your baby grows up a little, and then you'll be able to go back to work," I suggested kindly.

"No, we had a row yesterday." Emily's beautiful, full lips twitched in pain. "He made it clear that now I was a mother, he didn't want me to ever work again, even when our daughter will grow up!

"'Do you want people to think I can't provide for you and my daughter?' he asked angrily. When I tried to argue, he shouted, 'It's simply not done.' The very same words my mother used on the fateful *Night of the Staircase*." She started sobbing quietly.

"Do I ask him to leave his job because little Anette is born? How unfair men can be! Mother was right. It's a man's world, and we women are forced to become helpless bystanders chained by pots, pans and diapers!"

"Don't worry, Emily," I comforted her, taking her small dainty hand in my own, and patting it gently, "you will work; in your home and outside of your home too, if you want to. You will always work."

"But how?" she cried, looking at me with a startled look.

I smiled at her reassuringly, "When the time comes, you'll know how."

A few days later she left the hospital with her husband David tenderly holding baby Anette, both proud of their fine baby. I lost sight of Emily for a couple of years, until one day, I entered one of the big travel agencies in the center of Alexandria to get a train ticket. There was Emily, typing happily away and giving instructions to a new secretary.

"How did you convince David?" I asked, relieved to see her so active and happy.

"I told him about the *Night of the Staircase*, my own private 'epiphany,' and that from that night onwards my work and my job had become part of me. He could either have both parts or none. He chose both," she smiled merrily. "He understood that if I did not feel fulfilled we would both lose and pay in disappointment and discontent. You were right, Sister Thea, when you told me not to worry, and that I would always work. I didn't have the chance to tell you then, but your firm words were for me like an injection of energy and hope. I never forgot what you said. When I left the hospital with my baby girl Anette, I already knew, deep in my heart, that you were right and that I would indeed find a way to return to my job. You have since then, dear Sister Thea, always been a 'role model' in my life."

"I'm glad my injection worked," I laughed, "but you, yourself, Emily, were the main ingredient." Emily flashed her beautiful smile, and her happiness lit a flame of joy in my heart. Again, I was presented with a living proof of the magic of the right word in the right place; and the importance of the solidarity and moral support among women. Since we will have to pay a price for everything we leave undone, and for every life lived in vain, we should pluck up each other's courage to live meaningful and full lives and attempt to boost our finest, kindest and most useful selves.

12

VIRGIN

We had many Arab patients at the Jewish Hospital in Alexandria. One I will never forget is Mounira, a beautiful fourteen-year-old girl from one of the villages near Alexandria. She had soft dark brown curly hair, big brown velvety eyes, and full heart-shaped lips, which seemed to pout in silent protest, even when she slept. Fahed, her uncle on her mother's side, was our cook's helper. He brought her in late one night, with a serious hemorrhage.

"What happened to her?" I asked in consternation after the doctor had examined her, and I was told to give her an injection. "Was she raped?" Fahed's head drooped, and he murmured between his lips in confusion, "No, no rape, Schwester. She was virgin; it was her wedding night."

"Wedding night? But this girl is a child, and she has been cruelly mutilated! It's a case for the police," I said.

"No, Schwester, no police. It's custom, you see. It's custom in the village," he explained, while his dark eyes looked at me imploringly. "Her husband perforated her with finger bandaged with handkerchief, to show she virgin. But after he done it, and showed to all that she virgin," Fahed related unhappily, "Mounira fainted, and her blood started flowing nonstop, like water in canal of our village."

I felt faint myself and thought I would be sick. I couldn't believe what I had just heard. Fahed nodded unhappily, his imploring eyes shifting from the now sleeping Mounira to my face. I realized with sinking heart that what he had related was true! It had really happened, in the twentieth century! Not in the Middle Ages. "Don't you realize, Fahed, that if you hadn't brought her when you did, the girl would have died?" I asked.

"This is why I brought her to you," he said, lowering his head.

"But how could her husband treat her so cruelly?"

"It is because of his sister Latifa," Fahed said simply. I looked at him in amazement.

"What has his sister to do with this? How dare she interfere?"

"She didn't. Latifa, she dead."

I was becoming more and more confused. "Dead?" I almost shouted. I felt myself part of some farcical tragedy.

"How did she die, for goodness sake?"

"Drowned by her father. In the village pit."

"But why?" I asked in exasperation.

"Because on her wedding night, Latifah was found not virgin. On the handkerchief no blood on it, Schwester. Out of shame for the whole family her father drowned her. Khalil did not want Mounira's father to drown her, like his sister Latifah. He loves Mounira. That's why he plunged into her with his finger deep to make sure the handkerchief would come out with blood on it. When they saw the soaked hand-kerchief, all the snake-tongues in the village were immediately silent. They all saw Mounira is very virgin."

"He almost silenced Mounira, too!" I said bitterly. "Forever! That man should go to prison!"

"No, no Schwester," Fahed begged, "Khalil has to take care of Mounira now." I saw his point, and left the room in despair.

***

Mounira quickly recovered and was a delightful patient. She sang and danced with great charm and made everybody smile. She volunteered to help, and became a charming and diligent food distributor. When her forty-year-old husband, Khalil came to take his child-bride from the hospital back to the village, a week later, she refused to go with him and hid under my bed in my room. I at last found her there, but she looked at Khalil in fear and clung to me trembling and pleading, "Please let me stay at the hospital. I'll help you clean, cook, anything you say, Sister Thea, I'll do whatever you want me to do. Please let me stay here!" It pained me deeply to see the fear in her pleading black eyes, as she stooped quickly again and this time hid under my desk.

"Be good to her, Khalil," I said. "She's just a child." The

abashed bridegroom nodded and waited silently at the door of my room. I then opened my drawer and gave Mounira something she especially liked, a red lollipop. It did the trick. She came out from under my desk, smoothing her lovely, dark curly hair and she smiled at me showing a row of perfect white teeth. She eventually consented to go with Khalil, sucking her lollipop quite happily.

"And when you come to see me in the village, as you have promised me, Sister Thea, can you please bring me two lollipops, a red one and a golden one?"

I promised, and smiled at her with a heavy heart. Every month after that, I sent Mounira two big lollipops, a red one and a golden one.

***

I hear that this cruel and debasing custom of checking if the bride is a virgin on the wedding night, and if she has been duly circumcised, is still prevalent in several parts of the Middle East. I hope that this horrible custom will be abolished soon, together with *clitorectomy*, the inhuman circumcision of girls, and that both customs will be buried in the dust heap of nonuse before the end of our twentieth century. Women from democratic and more progressive countries should help their unfortunate Muslim sisters all around the world, to liberate themselves from these debilitating and crippling customs, that make out of girls and women invalids for life.

13

THE NOWHERE MAN

My involvement with the saving of Jews from Nazi Europe started with the "Nowhere Man." One of the several famous amusement localities in Alexandria in the years 1933 to 1945 was the Femina Bar at the Ramleh Railway Station. It was especially famous for its excellent dancers. Most of these dancers were either from Hungary or Rumania; and they usually had a residence permit for a period from three to six months. Many of them were fugitive Jews, and they all hoped to find a way not to have to return to Europe because of the growing climate of anti-Semitism. Most of them at length, found their way to the Hospital of the Jewish Community, for one reason or another, either being in need of medical treatment, or to ask us for advice and help concerning the possibility of staying in Egypt after ending their commitment to the owner of the Femina Bar.

We indeed found solutions for many of them, especially for the women dancers. They were mostly young professionals, in their early twenties, attractive, well-educated and honest. The best way to get a new residence permit was to find an Egyptian Jewish husband for them or a fictitious would-be husband who was not yet married and who was willing to perform a "white-wedding."[5] In both cases the Jewish community board paid the required customary "dowry," or the fictitious one. We also always tried to find for these women some kind of job, either in their artistic professions, or as secretaries, housekeepers, companions for elderly people, or dressmakers. They were generally satisfied with their situations, and many of them helped their families in Rumania or Hungary to join them, which in many cases saved their lives. I did my best to help the families too to find jobs and housing and to integrate them into the community. There were even quite a few "white-weddings" with a real happy end.

In the winter of 1934, among these dancers was a mixed couple from Germany. Karl was a Jew and Elizabeth was a Christian. They were friends, but not married or in love. For Karl, it was absolutely impossible to return to Germany because of the so-called "race disgrace"; and they too asked us for help. But before we found a solution for their problem, an Englishman who lived in Alexandria fell in love with Elizabeth, proposed to her, and was accepted. After her

---

5   A white-wedding was a phony wedding, which was cancelled after the non-Egyptian partner got her papers. The Egyptian partner sometimes was paid a fee, called a "dowry," for his services.

wedding, she stopped dancing, which caused Karl's dance career to come to an end. He did not succeed in becoming a solo dancer, and he couldn't find a suitable woman partner in Alexandria. He often came to talk to me about his tragic situation, and we became good friends.

When Karl's visa was due to expire he was very miserable, and he came to ask my advice at the hospital. I suggested that he should try his luck elsewhere. He agreed, and bought a train ticket for Khartoum, in Sudan, and I arranged with the man in charge of the sleeping carriage, whom I knew well (as his wife had been treated at our hospital), to hide Karl in his cabin, because he had no passport. Karl eventually found a job as a barman in Khartoum and did very well there. He wrote me warm letters of gratitude for some time, then the letters stopped, and I lost trace of him.

Months later, we got a phone call from Khartoum. The caller told Dr. Katz that he would send him a very sick man on the Khartoum-to-Cairo bound train, and that he had to be immediately hospitalized. "Could you please order an ambulance for the next day, to be waiting at the Sidi-Gaber train station?" the man asked anxiously over the phone. No name was mentioned. We knew that a small number of Jews lived in Khartoum, but we also often received Sudanese patients.

When the patient arrived I was shocked to see it was my friend Karl, the dancer from the Femina Bar. He was in a very bad state, and suffered from a severe infection in both legs. We were all very sorry to see him in such a condition. The doctors, after having examined him, had no other choice but to amputate one of his legs in which gangrene had set in. I quickly informed Elizabeth, his former dance partner, and she and her husband were at his bedside day and night. It took many weeks until he recovered. We ordered an artificial leg for him and we taught him painstakingly how to walk with it. He was a clever pupil, and learned quickly. It was sad to see this once excellent dancer trying to become a one-legged walker. In time, he became such an expert that when he drew himself up to his full height and clasped his hands firmly behind his back, looking up into the distant sky, he seemed to be an athlete and not a cripple. An expert dancer always knows how to dance his way through life, I thought.

Again, we had the same problem with him, but now it was still more complicated: How could we help him stay in Egypt without papers? And how could we start him on a more or less normal life? At least nobody had come from the authorities to ask for him. He was really a 'Nowhere Man,' and probably nobody would every bother him.

"What would you like to do, Karl?" I asked him gently, knowing how limited his choices were now.

"I am a good cook," he answered hesitatingly in his deep soft voice, "and what I would really like is to open a boarding house for students. If the Jewish community would finance me, I'm sure I could make a good job of it. With your kind encouragement Thea, I feel I can achieve anything."

"I'll put it before the board," I promised him, "at their very next session." He looked at me with a hopeful look in his steady gray eyes. I went to the Finance Committee of the

Alexandria Jewish board immediately and explained to them that the enterprise was worthwhile as Karl was a very bright and capable man despite his disability. I was so glad when they approved the project, and told them how grateful I was that they were always so understanding and generous. Without the benevolent help of the Egyptian Jewish community to these poor refugees from Europe, Karl and many like him would have been lost.

"There are thousands like me out there trying to flee from the Nazi Dragon who wants to gobble them up for his breakfast, Thea," Karl said sadly, and he pleaded in a trembling voice, "try to save them, Thea. What you did for me you can do for others too." I solemnly promised Karl that we would all do our best to save our brothers and sisters from the Nazi Hell in Europe. And this is how our "Rescue Committee for Jews from the Holocaust" started. Again, it was a case of the right words in the right place, and this time from kind-hearted and wise Karl. I felt that my conscience was pricked and invigorated by his encouraging words, and its willingness to help, grew strong and effective wings, which often helped me to soar up high in extremely hard moments, over every thorny calamity in the way.

Karl found a large apartment in the middle of town, and it didn't take long until all the rooms were rented. He was happy and enjoyed the work with the students. He became a warm father to them, and they became truly attached to him. His boarding house became a model one, cozy, orderly, beautifully decorated, clean and well furnished. His students became his family; and he helped them morally and even sometimes financially. Many of them said that if it were not for Karl they would not have been able to finish their studies.

We remained good friends to the end. Karl always offered me an excellent meal from his "Haute Cuisine," whenever I went to see him. He was a real *cordon bleu,*' and the students felt very lucky when they could book a room in his exclusive boarding house or rather 'home.' One of his students told me admiringly, "Karl is like a big bird winging over high mountains of wisdom and goodness, looking after us students trying to work hard in the serene valleys he always keeps lush, fresh and wholesome for us. If there were many people like Karl, the world would surely be a better place to live in." On hearing his appreciative words, I felt ripples of gladness flowing down my spine, like frothy waves splashing on turquoise-blue seas.

My contact with Karl was broken off after I left for Tiberius at the outbreak of the hostilities in 1947. There was no way to get any news from him then, because Egypt, like some other Arab countries, had declared war on Israel. Hopefully he was not bothered at all by the authorities, and continued to lead a normal, useful, and full life. Is the 'Nowhere Man' still in Egypt, I wonder? Perhaps these pages will bring him back to me.

Goldshmidt - the Redgen
Nurse Goldshmit, Head of the Rengen Dept.
Thea in the middle,
and Sister Lotte, the Head Nurse of the Internal Department.

14

MRS. HENNY

After the episode with the Nowhere Man, we succeeded in saving thousands of Jews fleeing from Europe. The word got around that we were eager to help and summons for aid reached us continuously. I recall a particularly unusual drama, of quite a different kind, which occurred in March 1938. It was a regular morning in our busy outpatient poly-clinic. At the end of a bench sat a middle-aged woman and beside her, two young boys. Then her turn came, and Dr. Levy's nurse let her into his clinic.

"Neither I nor my boys are in need of treatment, doctor," she said, and paused. "Are you the doctor from Germany?" she raised her eyes and asked suspiciously. The doctor on duty, who was an Egyptian Jew, said he wasn't and he accompanied her to Dr. Katz's office. I was then in charge of taking the preliminary details of patients. She gave her name as Mrs. Henny; she was Jewish and came from Berlin.

"These two boys are my children," she said. "My husband was a carpet dealer. When the Gestapo forced an entry into our apartment in January 1938, he got a heart attack, fell on the floor and died. They kicked him hard with their boots to make sure he was dead, and then stole everything: carpets, valuables, money. I tried to stop them but they beat me up before my two screaming children and hit them, too, and then left the apartment. What could I do? I knew they would soon come back. I left my poor dead husband in the apartment, took a few belongings and some hidden money, and ran away with my two boys. Now at last, I'm here in Alexandria, and in need of everything. This is why I came to you. Can you please help me?" She looked at me with imploring eyes.

"How did you find us?" I was intrigued.

"I met a kind Egyptian traffic policeman, and he told me only you can help me. The hospital is a well-known address for helping refugees."

"And how did you get to Alexandria?" I asked.

"I can't tell you about it," she said hesitatingly. "I don't remember, and I don't really want to . . .."

Her tone indicated it was no use to insist on further details. I looked at her searchingly. She was a pretty woman, in her forties probably. He hair was dyed blonde, and she wore black shining shoes with very high heels. Her tight, bright dress had a very large décolleté; her fingernails were painted bright red; and her large luminous green eyes were made up with black mascara.

We had some mixed feelings about her; but had pity on her and on her two sons, who sat quietly all the time, without uttering a word. We gave her enough money to live on for about a week and the address of an apartment dealer. She told us that for the time being she lived in a boardinghouse somewhere in town.

"What is your address?" I asked.

"I don't remember the exact address," she answered abruptly and pouted her lips, in a way which seemed to say, even if I remembered I wouldn't tell you.

Did she suffer from amnesia? I wondered. I listened to what she said, but was in doubt whether what she told us was the entire truth and, had an uncanny feeling that she was hiding something from us. I gave her the address she asked for, of the Jewish school for her boys and added gently, "Come back in case you need something else." She thanked me, and they left the hospital.

This strange scenario was a riddle to us; but they were refugees, and we felt we had to help them. Maybe they were still under shock because of all that had happened to them. "We shall wait and see," I told Dr. Katz, and he nodded his approval.

A few days later Mrs. Henny came back, without her children this time. "I found a small apartment," she said, "and my boys are already going to school. Thank you for your help, Sister Thea."

"There is no cause to thank me," I said, "I'm only doing my duty."

"Can you give me the address of your new apartment please?" I asked her. I was surprised by her immediate reaction.

"No, oh, no!" she jumped up in alarm. He face was flushed, and her green eyes fiery.

"But why not?" I asked her in amazement.

She hesitated a moment, then said confusedly, "I don't know the address of the apartment by heart yet." She lowered her eyes and added, "But I need some more money. This is why I came."

Once more I had an uneasy feeling about her, but gave her again a certain amount of money, and then asked her, "What kind of work are you able to do, so that we can recommend you, or perhaps even give you a job at the hospital?"

"Oh, no!" she nearly shouted. "I can't work, I don't want to do menial work, I simply don't know how to work. I have never worked in all my life!" She eventually calmed down, took her purse, and left.

From then on she came once a week at the same early hour in the morning, sat on a chair, and waited silently to get her weekly amount. She never liked to be questioned, and never offered any information on how she and the boys felt, or if she was in need of something additional to the small weekly amount she got from us. When I inquired, she always said, "I and my boys are all right, thank you very much." And that was all. She went away without any other comment. She always wore the same outfit, the same low-neck dress, high-heeled shoes, dyed hair and red fingernails. She was never sick, nor were her boys. However, she kept coming back every week, and continued to be a complete riddle to us for a long time.

In the meantime, her sons grew up. They left the Jewish

elementary school, and she asked us to find an apprenticeship for them in a factory. We got them a job at the Egyptian Copper Works Factory, founded by a well-known German-Jewish industrialist who was a refugee too. He told us that everybody liked those two silent boys, who proved to be very good and conscientious workers. "But they are extremely quiet," their boss said in amazement. "They never say anything about their home or their mother, they go home together every day after work; they are never tired or sick and they never complain about anything. I wonder if the way the Gestapo treated their father, did this to them." However, though her sons earned salaries, Mrs. Henny continued to come once a week for her money. There were no changes either in her behavior, or in her way of dressing. She was still a puzzle to all of us.

One day something happened which finally opened our eyes, and we suddenly found the explanation. She was practicing the world's oldest profession! One of our doctors saw her one morning in town walking up and down in a provocative manner on the street. She finally approached a man, talked to him, took his arm in hers, and quickly walked away with him. The riddle of Mrs. Henny was solved. How was it that we had never thought about this? The next time she came, I told her that we had seen her in town, near the prostitute quarter of Claude Bey.

"Do you live somewhere there?" I asked her.

She became confused and flushed. "No, no, I don't live there," she shrieked. "It's a lie!" And she left the room abruptly. She turned around and shouted, "It's not me! This foolish doctor who thinks he saw me, saw somebody else...it's not me, d'you hear?"

But even after the confrontation her visits didn't stop. She continued to come more or less regularly, took the money, and quickly left. And then suddenly she stopped coming. We knew from her sons at the factory that their mother was all right, but that she was no more in need of help from us, because they earned enough now and could help her out.

As time passed, I had nearly forgotten her. But in 1944 I had to accompany a woman patient to a psychiatric clinic in Hellouan and had to stay with her for three days. One morning I made a round with my patient through the garden of the clinic, and suddenly Mrs. Henny walked silently toward us. She didn't recognize me, and I didn't talk to her, not wanting to embarrass her. She looked completely absentminded, and her eyes had the faraway look that people who have lost their memory have. I asked the psychiatrist in charge about her.

"She was admitted some weeks ago," he said, "an ambulance brought her here, but nobody accompanied her. Also nobody comes to visit her. Her fees are paid regularly, but I don't know by whom. She's a complete riddle to us."

So Mrs. Henny was still a riddle even in the psychiatry ward and it saddened me to see her sad plight. "Is there any hope of her becoming well?" I asked him anxiously.

"None whatever," he said in a definite tone. "The prognosis in her case is quite unfavorable, there is almost no hope for her to recover," he repeated.

I felt sorry for her. Should we have done more for her? I asked myself with a gnawing feeling of guilt. Her two sons had left for the United States and were well settled there. This we learned from the people at the Copper Works factory. Probably, they were the ones who sent the payments for their mother at the psychiatric clinic.

In 1945, after the end of World War Two, a man came to the hospital one day and asked about Mrs. Henny's whereabouts. "Who are you?" I asked him.

"I'm Henny's husband," he said. "I've just arrived from Germany."

"But she thought you were dead!" I cried in amazement.

"No. I didn't die then, that day when the Gestapo came to our apartment," he explained. "I was saved by a good friend, a doctor, who came to see how we were, and found me lying unconscious. I heard that Henny is still here in Alexandria, and I would like to take her back to Germany and try to build our life together again."

I sadly gave him the address of the psychiatric clinic in Hellouan, where I told him his wife was being treated, though I feared that he had arrived too late to save her. But I didn't tell him that. We asked him to come back and tell us about her, but he never did. We heard, later, that she hadn't recognized him at all, and that he sadly returned to Germany without her. I hope that he at least found his sons in America.

There were many more such dramas which occurred almost every day at our hospital. The Nazi venom followed these poor fugitives who were trying to remake their lives in faraway Alexandria and often choked them even there, despite all our efforts to help them. Every time I failed to save a life, the knowledge of my failure gave me guilty feelings, humbled me, melted my bones, shrieked in my ears, and made my teeth rock loosely in their gums. At least we succeeded in saving the two boys, I tried to steady my breath, and to console myself.

Thanks to Thea Wolf from the Grand Rabbi Ventura

15

SHANGHAI SHIPS

Starting 1937, Italian passenger ships sailing from Trieste or Venice to Shanghai, carried Jewish refugee passengers who were running away from Nazi Germany and Europe. All those passenger ships made stopovers in Port Said for a few hours before sailing on.

One day, Dr. Katz received a letter from a friend by the name of Wilhelm Goldfarb, informing him he would be in Port Said on July 7, 1937 for a few hours on his way to Shanghai, which was at that time still part of Chiang Kai-shek's China. The Chinese Government had generously opened its gates to the fleeing Jewish refugees and had declared they would be welcome to settle in Shanghai. Wilhelm said he would be happy if the doctor could meet him on the ship. Dr. Katz traveled to Port Said, boarded the ship, and met his long-lost friend Wilhelm. The reunion was moving to both of them, and Wilhelm said wistfully that he would like to remain in Egypt if it was possible. Dr. Katz made some quick inquiries and Wilhelm's request was bluntly refused, and he sadly sailed on to Shanghai.

When he came back to Alexandria, Dr. Katz told us about his impressions and what he had seen and heard on the ship while he was there. There were whole families with their old parents and their children, singles, pregnant women, sick people--all of them relieved to be safe from the danger of Nazi Germany, but worried about traveling to an unknown land with such a different culture, and an uncertain future. Many of them were without sufficient means in order to find shelter in Shanghai and to build their lives again, as they had had to leave in a hurry and couldn't take anything with them. He also informed us that many of the refugees preferred to remain in Egypt if it were possible.

As a result, we decided to request from the Egyptian authorities that they allow some refugees to land in Port Said, and were fairly successful in several cases. We also visited every ship sailing to Shanghai and tried to give the refugees as much help as possible. We gave some money to many of them out of the hospital funds, so that they could feel a little bit more secure during their first days in China. We formed three groups: one in Cairo, one in Alexandria, and one in Port Said, so that every ship which laid anchor in Port Said was visited by a delegation from the Jewish hospitals, and we tried with the consent and even the help of the Port Authorities, to help those poor helpless fugitives as much as we could.

This benevolent activity went on until the day on which Mussolini declared war on the Allies and signed his infamous pact with Hitler. Generally, every week two or three ships had passed by Port Said, carrying approximately 20,000 Jewish refugees. On nearly every ship there were a few very sick people, and for them it was sometimes a question of life and death not to continue their journey. We were most often able to disembark these very sick people, and did not encounter any serious difficulties from the port authorities. The sick were then either hospitalized at the Jewish Hospital in Cairo or in our hospital in Alexandria. After their recovery, we tried to find a way for them to stay in Egypt until the end of the war, and then helped them emigrate to their relatives in Palestine. Unfortunately, it also sometimes happened that the patient did not recover, and we had to bury them at the Jewish cemetery in Alexandria or Cairo, run by the local community.

The Jewish community had generously allotted for this purpose a special place for the burial of refugees, and every tomb had a fine, marble tombstone bearing all the details we knew about the deceased. We took charge of their belongings, which we all forwarded at the end of the war to their families, sometimes by means of British, Australian, South African, or American soldiers, both Jews and non-Jews. Apart from one wedding ring, which was not delivered for unknown reasons by a woman who traveled to Australia, all the personal belongings of these deceased refugees arrived safely at their destinations.

When Mussolini entered the war, there were no more Shanghai bound passenger ships to Port Said. Unfortunately, our benevolent 'rescue and aid action' came to a halt. There was no more reason for me to travel to Port Said, where I had enjoyed for about three years, whenever I had to stay overnight, the warm hospitality of a gentle Jewish couple by the name of Yishai. I heard they live happily in Israel with their children and grandchildren, and several of the Shanghai bound Jews--while Mussolini is long dead.

16

HUMAN CARGO RESCUE

One hot humid day in the early summer of 1939, a policeman came to the door of the operating room, accompanied by a foreigner in civilian clothes. The policeman asked to speak to the *Rais*, the chief surgeon, explaining that the foreigner, whose name was Mark, wanted to tell him something. I told them they could speak freely to me, and I would report it to Dr. Katz.

Mark told me he was a sailor from the crew of the German freighter *Cairo*, which was due to sail back to Hamburg the following morning. All the ship's cargo had been unloaded at various Mediterranean ports--except for its human cargo. This was a group of German Jews, who had embarked in Hamburg in the hope of finding refuge from the Nazis in one of the Mediterranean ports. But every time the vessel had docked at a port, the ship's captain, who was a Nazi, had locked them in their cabin, as he was determined to return them to a concentration camp in Germany.

The thirteen people, the young sailor said, were by now distraught and in total despair, knowing that they were doomed if they could not disembark in Alexandria, as it was the last port of call. He was so sorry for them that he felt impelled to do something. He had asked a policeman guarding the ship whether there were Jews in the city who could help. The policeman decided to bring him to the Jewish Hospital.

The sailor had an ingenious rescue plan. According to international maritime law, he told us, if an epidemic breaks out aboard a vessel anchored in port, the captain is obliged to inform the quarantine authorities, and the ship has to remain in port until it gets health clearance.

"If," he said, "these thirteen people were suddenly to be taken ill, the health authorities will have to be informed, a doctor will be sent aboard and will probably order them to be hospitalized. All one needed to do to make them appear sick," he said breathlessly, "is to give them a strong dose of sleeping pills."

"Wait," I said, "Dr. Katz has to approve of this." I introduced Mark and the kind policeman to Dr. Katz, and reported what they had told me.

"But how will you accomplish this plan?" Dr. Katz asked Mark.

"As it is part of my job to give the refugees their evening meal," Mark said, "I could tell them about the plan and make sure they took the pills. I would then inform the authorities about the epidemic and the thirteen-sick people would immediately be brought to the Jewish Hospital next morning." His voice was earnest, and his big blue eyes were imploring.

Dr. Katz asked me what I thought about this daring plan, and I immediately said that we should try it. We were all aware of the enormous risk we were taking, including the brave sailor, but he was quite confident that everything would work out. We provided him with the sleeping pills after asking him to tell us about the state of health and age of each person in the group. He knew them well, because they had been on the ship for more than four weeks, and he had become friends with them. Then I drove him and the policeman back to the docks, reminding him several times during the drive to make sure that each person put the pills in his or her mouth and swallowed them with some water. None of us connected with the rescue mission had much sleep that night. Too much was at stake. Thirteen human beings might be severely endangered if our plan went wrong.

The next day was a light one in the operating room, with only one case of minor surgery. We waited anxiously for a phone call from the quarantine authorities. Finally, it came at noon. Thirteen Jewish passengers aboard a German freighter were in deep comas after apparently taking an overdose of sleeping pills. Could we admit them all? Of course, we could.

We began to make immediate preparations for the necessary first aid, but it was four hours before they were brought to the hospital. All were still in a deep coma. They were weak already, and because they arrived at four o'clock instead of nine, as planned, most of them had developed severe lung infections. It took nearly two months to put them on their feet again. Guards were stationed at their bedsides all the time. The impatient and disappointed Nazi captain who came to take them back to the ship the next day was forced to leave without them.

Once they had recovered, they all expressed their desire to go to Palestine, where they had relatives. But how were we going to get them there? They had no immigration certificates or tourist visas for Palestine, and all our requests to the British authorities in Egypt were fruitless. It was clear that we would have to arrange for them to go illegally.

Once again it was the Egyptian police and the kind port authorities' personnel who came to the rescue. They proposed the following plan: since the group members were still technically prisoners of the port authorities, it would be possible to have them transferred to the port prison in Port Said. They would travel there by train from Alexandria in three reserved compartments, accompanied by a port police officer in civilian clothes and myself. In Port Said we would look for a large seaworthy fishing vessel licensed to fish to the edge of Palestinian territorial waters. The policeman and I would escort the "illegals" aboard a police patrol boat, and see that they were safely transferred to the fishing vessel that would sail them outside Egyptian waters.

The refugees were told of the plan and unanimously agreed to accept it. We had a go-between, by the name of Benny, for all matters concerning Jewish refugees. He came to Port Said with us together with two young brothers from Hungary and a pretty blonde girl from Czechoslovakia, named Maria.

The day we left the hospital the entire staff turned out to bid Godspeed to the group. They had been given warm clothes, money, and food. We arrived safely in Port Said and a police car took us all to the port prison. It was already about four o'clock in the afternoon, and everybody was exhausted. I wished each of the group a good night and told them that Benny, our go-between, had already hired a fishing boat belonging to an Italian, and that he had also rented a brand-new cutter to be used in case they were pursued by the British coastal patrols. They were all very calm, and I was proud of them. I reassured them (and myself) that all would be all right.

I returned to my hotel room, and then meticulously reviewed our plan and the schedule for the next day again. I also purchased watermelons, soft drinks, fruit, bread, butter, and cheeses, for all the refugees, including the three additional ones. These two Hungarian brothers and the girl from Czechoslovakia, with our help, had been hidden for several months in Alexandria. The secret police were frantically searching for them as they had arrived illegally, as many others at that time.

The next morning Benny and I went to the port prison, where all sixteen fugitives were waiting for us. A prison car drove us all to the police boat, and we sailed to the fishing vessel outside the port area. All the refugees boarded the ship joyfully. I hugged each of them and bid them farewell and I returned to the shore with fear and hope battling each other like stormy waves in my heart.

Back in Alexandria, we all waited anxiously for the news

that "your aunt has arrived," which was our secret motto. We had to wait for a nerve-racking week for the message. Finally, we received a full report from Maria, who wrote to us from Palestine. She told us in her letter that a British coastal patrol had detected the fishing boat on the second day out, not far from Jaffa, whereupon the refugees abandoned the vessel and took to the cutter. The sea was rough, and it was only thanks to the three-young people who manned the oars that the cutter managed to make the beach at Tel Aviv on the third day. They were met on the shore by Hagana members, and then were taken to a *kibbutz* (a collective farm), and given shelter until their relatives arrived to welcome them.

We immediately passed on the good news to the port officer, without whose help those poor, destitute people would have been taken back to an extermination camp in Germany. We also notified the policeman who had brought the brave German sailor to us, and he rejoiced to hear that the rescued refugees were safe in Palestine.

Due to this marvelous and courageous collaboration between Jews and Arabs to save Jews from the Holocaust, as related above--it was always clear to me that the Israel and Egypt peace treaty, signed fifteen years ago, after thirty years of conflict in the Middle East, would be proved successful. Today it serves as a precedent and model to the whole of the Peace Process in the region. It is good today to remember again the crucial and generous help the Egyptians extended to the Jewish refugees fleeing from the Nazi Holocaust, more than half a century ago. This unusual historic fact concerning the Jewish-Moslem collaboration in Egypt is still quite unknown, and it may constitute a further link in strengthening the growing peace ties between Jews and Arabs in the Middle East. Furthermore, this collaboration illuminates an aspect of the resistance against the Nazis and the Holocaust which has not been described before, and it certainly should be known. Past collaborations between Jews and Arabs, especially on such a delicate subject, render the prospect of present and future ones more tangible, hopeful and still more promising--with peace, the whole of the Middle East could become a '*pomegranate*,' the Biblical symbol of plenty.

17

WORLD WAR TWO
IN ALEXANDRIA

With the outbreak of World War Two, our hospital admitted Allied soldiers. Among them, we had South Africans (black and white), Free French soldiers and officers, Yugoslavs, Poles, and Czechoslovakians. From 1940, the town of Alexandria, especially the port area and the railroad to Cairo, became a nightly target for bombs---first by the Italian air force and later by the German Luftwaffe. They also bombarded civilian targets indiscriminately, and we had to work very hard to treat the wounded, nonstop all day and night. These were mostly civilians who were the victims of the falling bombs and shells that had hit them in their homes, before they had time to reach the shelters or the beaches where they ran to hide.

Many people erroneously thought that because sacks of sand were put before the doors of buildings, they would be

safer on the sands of the beaches, where they ran in multi-
tudes to hide from the bombs. This was where they were
killed off like flies, especially around the port area. It was
a heartbreaking sight to see whole families--grandparents,
wives and children killed or wounded, and many among
them mutilated for life. With every life, we couldn't save we
hated Hitler still more. Many were killed by the shells in their
own houses and never reached the Hospital. I pitied those
poor, innocent people who were the victims of this atrocious
war. People who went to sleep the night before in their cozy
beds, would never wake again, those who expected to rise
and run to their work, will not rise, their beds became their
cooling boards and their blankets became their shrouds.

During all that time, all the hospitals of the Alexandria
area were on nonstop duty. In addition to the multitude
of people who had to be hospitalized; many others got
first-aid treatment and were sent home, after the shrieking
clear-out sirens were heard. There were often cases where
people couldn't go back home because their homes had been
bombarded and completely destroyed and we kept them at
the hospital until we could send them to relatives or friends.
During one of those terrible bombing nights, the hospital was
badly hit, and all the walls of the operating ward collapsed
while we were giving first aid to about seventy severely
wounded civilians and soldiers. But we calmly and courageously continued our work behind dark heavy curtains in
order to obey the blackout orders.

Will there always be wars? I asked myself in despair. Will
humanity ever be able to blot out this terrible concept from

its historical dictionary? World War One was supposed to be the war to end all wars, and here we were in the midst of a dreadful World War Two, more horrible still than its predecessor! Will it ever end? Will humans learn one day not to butcher each other and find a way to live in peace with each other? I craved to take war by the tail, as boys did to dead rats, and fling it deep into the ocean to drown it forever. I hated war with all my heart and considered it my own personal enemy. I will fight against war as long as I live, and as long as it hasn't been banished from the earth, I promised myself solemnly on that fateful El Alamein night, when Rommel was at our door. An icy shiver traveled down my spine then, and remained there since, to remind me of my promise, whenever I became lax and was sidetracked by lesser important issues.

I discovered the same fervent hatred of war in the poetry of the excellent British peace poet Wilfred Owen, who died in the trenches in the First World War, when he was only twenty-five years old. In his beautiful antiwar poetry, he wrote about the abominable absurdity of war, and he moved me deeply with his strong feelings about the "pity of war" and his protest "for those who die as cattle." I closely identified with his words, and hoped for the requiem of the death of the whole concept of war, as well as the practice of warfare. His moving and tantalizing words, "I am the enemy you killed, my friend," in his beautiful and moving poem, "*Strange Meeting*," have remained fresh in my mind as when I first read them.

Every night we went on treating wounded civilians at

our hospital, and also wounded Allied soldiers, who were later transferred to military hospitals in Alexandria and Cairo. The German Luftwaffe joined the Italian air force fully, and the bombings became still heavier, and the losses as well. This went on until the Allied forces' counter-offensive at El Alamein and the chasing of what remained of Rommel's army through the Libyan Desert. Hitler had given strict instructions to Rommel not to retreat, and to advance to victory. However, Rommel saw that he stood no chance against Montgomery and he countermanded Hitler's orders. This made Hitler very angry and it broke their friendship, which eventually led to Rommel's rebellion and plot against Hitler's life. When Hitler found that out, he forced Rommel to poison himself. And all that began at El Alamein.

The El Alamein campaign started in the late afternoon. We suddenly heard faraway shots and the booming of cannons--a whole ugly shrieking symphony of war. We all went up to the roof of the hospital, and with the help of binoculars we could distinguish the deadly multicolored fires of the enemy. It was a frightening sight. Because of "him" (surely war must be masculine), people had to go down into the shelters, and often to sleep there all night, trembling with fear. In the crowded shelters children and women wept and old people groaned with fear. Not only Europe, but Alexandria too was in mourning. Usually, in the summer, tourists from abroad and from Cairo had filled the sunny, golden-sand beaches; now the beaches were drab and empty. Some courageous families from Cairo had tried to come for a few days to enjoy the bathing as they did every year, but their children shrieked so much from fear at night during the bombardments that they quickly returned to Cairo. Some of these children later suffered from bombardment syndromes and were treated at the Hospital. Others continued to have nightmares all their lives.

There were many British, American, Australian, South African and Jewish Brigade soldiers in the front lines of El Alamein, and several of them, before leaving for the front, had left their personal belongings with us, hoping to take them back after the end of the battle. About a week after the battle, we were called to the entrance of the hospital, where we met only a few of them again. The rest had died heroes' deaths on the battlefront of El Alamein. There had been heavy losses during the battle, and among the dead were many of the young men who had given us their personal belongings before leaving for the front. We sent these items back after the end of the war to their bereaved families, with letters of condolences, sorrowfully relating our last memories of their wonderful young boys. What a pity, what a dreadful pity, so much precious blood spilled in the sands, my sorrowful heart wept in me, though I always tried to keep a calm countenance, so as not to influence the staff's morale.

We knew that the Allied forces were advancing, and the whole of Alexandria became an enormous military camp. The Jewish community put all its human resources at the disposal of the Allied soldiers. Several military clubs for the soldiers of the Jewish Brigade and others were opened, and these functioned day and night. The center of all human activity was now mainly the welfare of the soldiers. If we Jews in Egypt were still alive, it was only thanks to them. Later, we learned that every Jew living in Egypt was listed on that detailed "Death List" found on Rommel's superintendent's body. We felt deep gratitude for those courageous young men of the Allied Forces, who safeguarded our lives, often at the cost of their own lives. What a pity, what a terrible pity, my heart wept in me and shrieked in my bones.

18

LIBYAN WIDOWS

One morning at about five o'clock, I was called to come at once to the hospital, because there was a truck outside waiting to enter the hospital grounds with many people on it. I quickly ran to the front gate and found a heavy truck with about thirty women, talking a kind of Arabic which I did not understand. Two Allied soldiers who accompanied them informed me that these were Jewish women from Benghazi, Libya. They had been rescued when the Nazis invaded Benghazi and had been brought through the whole Libyan Desert and were to be sent on to Palestine.

"But they are terribly tired and exhausted," one of the soldiers said. "Could you please take charge of them for a while before they continue their trip? I am afraid that many of them will die on the way if they don't get help and nourishment."

"Of course, of course, come in please, *Shalom Aleikhem,*

welcome, welcome!" I told these poor women, and they smiled faintly at me. We fed them, clothed them, treated the ones that needed treatment, and let them rest on stretchers which we quickly prepared in our ambulatory ward. I clearly remember them--young, beautiful women with brightly colored shawls over their heads, and big, black shining eyes. They didn't stay long, only one night, but our hearts warmed up to them, and I will never forget them. They told us, weeping all the while, that their husbands, fathers and brothers had been taken away by the Nazis. Every male in their families that was older than thirteen, was arrested by Hitler's Gestapo, cruelly beaten and driven away to concentration camps in Poland.

"Don't cry. I'm sure you'll see your husband and son again." I tried to comfort a delicate, pale young woman who was silently crying. She looked like a Madonna in her black veil, as she gazed at me with her big velvety eyes through her tears. Her slight shoulders shivered under her veil.

"Thank you, *infermiera* (sister)," she said softly. "God bless you, and may He listen to you."

They were taken away the next day in the same truck, to Palestine. It was a "gone with the wind" war event. We never heard of them again. Did they ever see their husbands and sons again? I hope that at least some of them did; though I later heard that the Jews from Libya had been taken to Auschwitz, and were among the first who died there, like flies, not being used to the bitter cold and the drastic conditions in the camp. Those who survived the cold and hunger, found their deaths in the gas chambers. Dr. Mengele had a special abhorrence for the Jews from Arab Lands, as he saw in them a twice Semitic tribe. He often did not even have them selected, but just sent the whole trainloads straight to the gas-poisoned showers. He treated the Greek Jews from Salonika in much the same way. Only three percent of the Jews from Libya and from Salonika survived the atrocities of the war. This historic fact concerning the sorrowful fate of the Mediterranean Jews, both the Libyan and the Greek, is not known enough, and should be more researched.

19

FUGITIVES

During all that war period our polyclinic went on opening its doors to the public every day, except on the Sabbath when it was closed during the morning hours. More than a hundred regular patients were treated daily even then, in addition to the hundreds of wounded soldiers. The fee continued to be one Egyptian piaster, which was a symbolic fee, and it included treatment and medication.

We also accepted patients from an UNRWA camp nearby, by the name of Tolombat. There were several thousand refugees in the camp, mostly from Yugoslavia, Czechoslovakia and Austria, and among them there were many Jews. Every day the ambulance brought patients from the camp, and the pregnant women delivered their babies at our hospital. Many of these refugees later came to visit us on the days they had permission to leave the camp, as we were the only family they had.

Our hospital also continued to be a haven and a refuge for Jews from the whole of Europe, who had run away from the Nazi regime. They arrived destitute on the shores of Alexandria, where they were immediately taken into custody by the port police. But we had an arrangement with the prison officials, and as soon as they were in prison, a policeman was sent to the hospital to inform the *Rais*, the chief surgeon or myself, that there were Jews in prison. It was an act of pure human solidarity on the side of the Egyptian police, and we were very grateful to them for it. "*Ya sistte, Raissa*," the Egyptian policeman would say excitedly, "they are so miserable and forlorn, it breaks my heart; come with me and see them for yourself."

I drove with the policeman in my red Morris-Minor, which always caused a sensation in the streets in those days, as not many women drove then. I saw the pain and suffering of the poor fugitives, and always succeeded at length in getting permission from the prison officer in charge to bring the refugees to the hospital for treatment and hospitalization. The Egyptian people are kind and good-hearted, and the policemen couldn't witness so much pain without trying to help. Never was a refugee refused permission to leave the prison or the ship on which he arrived, sometimes as a stevedore.

During the hospitalization of refugees, a policeman was put on guard at their bedside day and night. The policeman got his meals like everybody else at the hospital; he also got some medicine for his family, and he himself was treated when he asked for it. Thus, he at length became a friend, and he always left the hospital with regrets when the time came for the refugee-patient to leave.

We found a solution for almost every refugee who was interested in remaining in Egypt or in going to Palestine. At the beginning of the Nazi period, many famous physicians arrived in Alexandria with no papers, or with a restricted tourist entry visa. This was often the first leg of their flight from Europe. We all put our time at their disposal and tried our best to help them before they continued to their next destination which unfortunately, was not always the last one for them. For several of them we found work either at our own hospital, or at the Jewish Hospital in Cairo, which had also gained a widespread reputation as an excellent hospital.

One day there arrived at our hospital a famous podiatrist from Berlin by the name of Dr. Kohn, with his wife Maria and daughter Ilse. He had an entry visa to Egypt, but no permission to practice medicine, though he was a well-known specialist for foot sickness, especially flat feet. Maria, a former pupil of the Academy of Arts in Vienna, opened a luncheon room, mostly for refugees, who often couldn't pay for their meals; Ilse made delicious cookies and *pralines*. And when all these jobs didn't suffice to make a living, they finally rented their flat to the then king of Greece and his family for a short while, and made plans for continuing their exile in South Africa. But Dr. Kohn became ill and suddenly died, and his sad wife eventually accepted a job at the YMCA in Minieh, Upper Egypt. She traveled from there to Khartoum, and in time became the head manageress of the entire women's household of the Mahdi of Sudan. Maria stayed there for three years, then returned to Alexandria with an enormous artistic collection of sculptures, including all those presented to her gratefully by the women of the Mahdi's Court. She eventually joined her daughter Ilse in Canada, where they probably both live to this day.

Then there was the story of Margot, one of the secretaries of our laboratory. We had to find several hiding places for her because the frontier police were chasing her as her papers were not in order. At length, we found what we were looking for, an Egyptian Jew who was a bachelor and an Egyptian citizen. This was no easy matter, because out of the 100,000 Jews living in Egypt in the forties, only about 5 percent were allowed the Egyptian citizenship, though many of them had been in Egypt for generations.

Joseph, the bachelor, accepted our proposal for a 'white wedding' with Margot for a high sum of money. But during a certain period, they had to live together under the same roof, because the border police suspected something fishy. Joseph, in spite of all his former assurances that he would stick to his side of the bargain, felt he was entitled to his normal claims concerning his so-called wife. Margot refused and ran away, and we had to find other hideouts for her. When Joseph realized that she had made it public that she didn't want to turn her white wedding into a 'black' one, as she put it, he stopped chasing her sexually. She could then hide in his house in peace without being molested anymore.

I remember several other refugee episodes, such as that of Leo. Leo was a young Jew, about eighteen years old, whom the crew of a German coal freighter discovered in a corner of the coal storing room of the ship when it arrived in Alexandria. I was informed of this unfortunate case by a kind customs officer. We got permission to enter the ship and to take the shivering stowaway to the hospital. He was as white as a sheet and suffered from a severe lung infection. When he finally recovered after several weeks of hospitalization, we at length, after countless efforts, managed to send him to Palestine where his father lived. This was done with the help of Ibrahim, an Arab railway conductor from Cairo to Lydda, who took pity on the young boy, and hid him in his railway cabin though he was endangering his post, and safely got him into *Eretz Israel*.

Not all the stories ended well. Mr. Hirsch, the director of the Egyptian Copper works in Alexandria, and his wife had a sadder story. This factory still exists to this day, but it is owned by the Egyptian government. The Hirschs had fled from Nazi Germany in 1938, then had to flee again when the Rommel army was on the outskirts of Alexandria. They escaped to Ethiopia, but came back to Alexandria after the war. Unfortunately, they had to uproot themselves and move again when President Nasser nationalized the factory and banished them.

"Our life is one long uprooting," Liese Hirsch told me sadly, her eyes brimming with painful tears. "We're so tired of being wandering Jews! We're not young anymore, and have worked hard all our lives, and now we have nothing again, and nowhere to go. Why does this happen to us again and again?" They tried to regain their property, but like most of the Jews in Egypt, they lost all their property.

Then there was Mrs. Resnick, a mother with two grown-up daughters. The three of them were mentally sick after what they had gone through in Germany, and we had to sustain them continuously. One daughter, the eldest, had to be hospitalized in a specialized Nerve Clinic, and we treated Mrs. Resnick and her younger daughter at our own clinic in the hospital. When the war ended and they were feeling better, after strenuous efforts, we managed to send them to Palestine illegally. In *Eretz Israel*, they gradually regained their balance and were able to live a normal, healthy and active life.

There were several other bright events, which crowned our efforts and brought much joy to our hearts: three weddings among emigrants, and some others between Jewish soldiers from *Eretz Israel* and Jewish refugee girls. This provided a solution for the girls, who happily accompanied their husbands back home. Otherwise, these refugees could not have immigrated to Palestine, as the British Mandate's "White Book," which controlled immigration to a minimum number, was in force then.

The Jewish sailors from the former Borchardt Line from Palestine often liked to come for a cup of coffee at our hospital whenever their ships were anchored in Alexandria port, and we always enjoyed chatting with them and listening to their exciting and stimulating stories about the *yishuv* in Palestine.

Even privates and officers, from the Polish, Czechoslovakian, and Yugoslavian exile armies were treated at our hospital. Some were hospitalized, and many others simply came for the company and the warm atmosphere at the hospital. The hospital, during those dark war years, was a real international microcosm and crossroad. It became a haven for all, in a town situated at the edge of the hellish war front of El Alamein.

20

GREEK OR GERMAN?

Mr. Rosenstein was our main hospital supplier. He was a German Jew from Frankfurt, where he was the co-owner of a well-known hospital supply factory, and he was also the main supplier for the Egyptian government hospitals. For years he visited Egypt regularly, at least once a year, and continued from there to Greece, where he also supplied hospitals. He happened to be in Alexandria at the outbreak of World War Two, and he was desperate, for his wife and little child were in Germany. We strongly advised him not to return there, but to try and find a way to save his wife and little Puzzi.

"You are right," Mr. Rosenstein said to me sorrowfully. "I'll try my best to work out something." His strong, tall, lithe body slouched sadly, his shoulders drooped and he seemed years older, "some nights I feel as if my brain will explode," he confided.

However, he did eventually find a solution. The way he

found to solve his dilemma was by means of a Greek passport. When he got it, Mr. Rosenstein became Mr. Rousso, born in Salonika, Greece. He traveled to Milan, contacted his wife, and told her to leave everything in Frankfurt and to join him, with Puzzi, in Milan. They joyfully met there, then travelled to Paris, where they waited for news from their relatives in the United States concerning an entry visa for the States.

However, this was not the end of their troubles. They escaped from Paris to Lisbon just a few minutes before the Germans entered Paris. In Lisbon, they waited and waited for their visa number to come up so that they could travel to the United States, but every time they went to the American embassy they got the same answer, "You have to wait for your number."

Mr. Rosenstein eventually decided otherwise. He had enough of waiting. He went to the Egyptian embassy in Lisbon, presented his Greek passport, and asked for a tourist visa for himself, his wife, and Puzzi. They were lucky and rapidly got it. They sailed from Lisbon to Trieste and waited there for an Egyptian ship to continue their voyage. For years Mr. Rosenstein had traveled with the same Egyptian ship, by the name of *Nil*. He was well known and appreciated by the whole crew, and by Hermann, the chief cook, who was a German. The *Nil* at length anchored in Trieste, and the Rosenstein family embarked. They had a pleasant voyage and arrived safely in Alexandria, where they came straight away to the hospital to meet us. We were very glad to see them safely among us.

"I told you I'd find a way, didn't I?" Mr. Rosenstein smiled his mischievous half-smile. I was so happy to see his twinkling blue eyes again; so was the entire hospital staff, which had heard about his misfortune. We noted that charming little Puzzi had her father's eyes and wise smile and her mother's beautiful blonde hair and cheerful nature.

They eventually rented a small apartment near the Alexandrian *Corniche* on the Mediterranean shores, and Puzzi went to *l'Ecole Françoise*. Mr. Rosenstein started a small business, and his wife Lotte began sewing icecaps and hot water bottles. They had a hard time, but never complained; they were happy to be safe and free in Alexandria.

Their happiness, however didn't last long. One morning the doorbell rang. Mr. Rosenstein opened it, and there were two policemen, who showed him an arrest order. He had been denounced as not being a Greek citizen, but a German citizen who had entered Egypt under false pretenses. He was imprisoned and told that he would be brought before a judge and exiled to Germany, together with his family. Lotte sorrowfully got in touch with us and informed us that her husband had been taken into custody, I could hear her trying to arrest her sobbing over the phone. It was heartbreaking.

We immediately went into action. We found out that it was Hermann, the German cook of the *Nil*, who had denounced them. The cook had become a Nazi party member, and in order to show his faithfulness to the Fuhrer, he had betrayed his old acquaintance, Mr. Rosenstein. He testified he was a German Jew who had always traveled with a German passport, and that his Greek passport was not a genuine one. The cook had deposited his declaration at the Alexandrian

Greek Consulate, with the same person who was in charge of all the foreigners residing in Alexandria. This man called Dimitri, was himself a Greek citizen and Mr. Rosenstein had obtained his Greek passport from him. When I went to see him, he promised us his help and he kept his promise.

Mr. Rosenstein was in prison for six weeks. He asked the prison guards for a job, and he got one; he had to clean a police station, not far from the hospital, every morning. Many of our staff passed this police station on their way to work at the time Mr. Rosenstein was outside cleaning the entrance of the station. Thus we got to see him and were sure that he was all right.

The day of the trial arrived. Luckily Mr. Rosenstein spoke Greek fairly well. Mr. Dimitri was called to testify whether Mr. Rousso was a Greek citizen or not. He declared that he was, that he had known him for many years, and that every time he came to Egypt for his business, he always presented himself at the Consulate with his Greek passport. The accusation was nullified, and Mr. Rosenstein was liberated immediately. He returned to his job and Lotte to hers; life went on as before. It was a great relief, and we were very grateful to Dimitri.

The Rosenstein's left Alexandria for Ismailia with us the night the German Messerschmitt's made direct hits at the water reservoir of Alexandria, and the Rommel motorcycle vanguards were already in a suburb of the town. They returned with us from Ismailia to Alexandria after the danger of the German Wehrmacht invasion had been checked by the Allies at El Alamein. However, the Rosenstein family's wanderings were not at an end. They had to leave Egypt in 1948 when the hundred thousand Egyptian Jews left or were exiled from Egypt. They found a permanent home in the newly born State of Israel, where most of the million Jews immigrated after they were exiled from the Arab countries. The Rosenstein's' wandering at last came to an end, as well as that of the Jews from the Arab countries, after two thousand years of exile. The 'wandering Jews' became pioneer Jews in the modern renascent Israel, that was the land of their ancestors in Biblical times.

21

TO ISMAILIA AND BACK

In midsummer 1942, when Rommel and his army were rapidly advancing through the Libyan Desert, the hospital received some more direct hits during a heavy bombing attack, and the entire wall of the operating Department crashed down again. We were then giving first aid treatment to about eighty wounded civilians, and some soldiers from India, belonging to the Sikh sect. I remember that they pleaded continuously, "Please don't cut my hair, please memsahib, don't make me sinful, don't cut my hair!" I abided by their request, and did not touch their long black curls under their white turbans.

The next day rumors spread through Alexandria that a spearhead of the German Wehrmacht was quickly advancing toward the town. It had already reached the outskirts of Mex, a suburb of Alexandria, and it was predicted that in no more than twenty hours the German Wehrmacht would enter Alexandria. There was great confusion and fear among the population, especially among the Jews, who had heard of the Nazi atrocities.

People started to leave Alexandria for Cairo or some other town in the Nile Delta. The hospital council decided to evacuate as many patients as possible, and either to send them home, or to send them to hospitals in Cairo, which was declared an "open city." Among the patients at our hospital then, in addition to the wounded soldiers, were bankers, writers, high school principals, actors, journalists, musicians and college professors. They were all sent back home to their families with medicine and prescriptions for a month of treatment, as well as minute instructions how to continue their treatment.

Among the hospital staff, there were several German Jews: four nurses, two secretaries of the laboratory, the chief surgeon, the chief physician, his assistant with his wife and a child, and the chief of the laboratory. We had earlier received a secret warning from a friendly Egyptian high official, whose seriously ill daughter had been successfully treated and healed at our hospital, that a detailed list of the Jewish refugees in Egypt was in the hands of the S.S. which accompanied the Rommel army. He told us there was a real danger for all of us, for if Rommel won, we would be arrested as soon as Alexandria was under German rule, returned to Nazi Germany, and taken to extermination camps. We all knew about the atrocities committed in these camps and fully understood what it meant.

I have often been asked, "How was it that in 1942 in Egypt you knew about the Nazi concentration camps, when most of the world still didn't?"

"Many refugees who arrived to our shores knew exactly what was happening there and made it known to us," I answered sadly. "Furthermore, I myself received urgent letters from my relatives in Sydney, informing me that my parents had been deported to the concentration camp in Lodz. They wanted me to help them. I tried hard to do so, but what could I do from here? I attempted everything, including pleading with the British authorities in Egypt, Cyprus and Malta, but nothing seemed to help..."

Three nurses who were good friends of mine also tried several times to help their parents who were still in Germany. Charlotte even went to Cyprus to represent us, and try there, but the British high commissioner in Cyprus just raised his brows and lifted his lean fingers helplessly in the air. The same happened with poor Clara and Ruth, who traveled all the way to Malta for the same purpose, but unfortunately, with the same results. We were all in despair.

We had a rapid refugee meeting at the hospital, and it was decided that we had to leave Alexandria as quickly as possible. Some of us went as far as Sudan; others went to Ethiopia, mainly to Asmara; and a small group was granted permission by the British to travel to Bethlehem, where they lived for a few months in a refugee camp. Dr. Fritz Katz, myself, another nurse, the head nurse of the Internal Wards, the secretary of the laboratory, the Rosensteins with ten-year-old Puzzi, and the chief manager of the Bata Shoe Shops in Cairo, decided to leave for Ismailia. In Ismailia, we had a good friend, a German Jew by the name of Herbert, who had served in a German submarine during World War One. Herbert now served in the Jewish Brigade, attached to the British army, and was in charge of the ammunition depot of the Ismailia area.

We traveled in two cars and took with us a small suitcase each of personal belongings. Everything else was left behind. We had decided to leave in the early morning and travel through side streets for reasons of safety, and because the main roads were completely blocked by General Wilson's Ninth Army coming from Syria. His destination was to reinforce Montgomery's Allied Forces at El Alamein.

At around four o'clock in the morning on the day of our departure, the German Spitfire airplanes stormed Alexandria, and the main waterworks were severely hit. As a result, a great part of the town was submerged, which made things still more difficult. Our departure point was the hospital. Our friends finally arrived, though it was very difficult for them to drive through the inundated streets. A hasty farewell party was arranged for us, in which we all drank a glass of Nile water, prepared by Mohammed, our helper in the operating room.

"There is an old Egyptian proverb which says: 'that he who drinks Nile water, shall always come back to Egypt,'" Mohammed said hopefully, his dark eyes shining sadly. We drank quickly, the water was pure and tasty; some of us had tears in our eyes.

"Will we really come back?" I wondered with a heavy heart.

We finally drove away after many *salaams* from the local

staff and workers, and good wishes for a safe arrival, and also for a safe return.

When we arrived at Benha, a large industrial town on the shores of the Nile and had to cross a bridge over the river, we suddenly heard a tremendous roar over our heads. There they were, the dark airplanes again, bombing the town and the bridge to which we had almost arrived, shells shrieked, and the skies were lit up by the explosions. Luckily the attack didn't last long, and most of the bombs fell into the Nile. We then hastily crossed the bridge and had a feeling of having crossed the fire line of hell itself. On our way, we passed many military ambulances full of wounded soldiers and civilians. They were mostly Free French soldiers who were wounded in the battle at Bir Hachim in the Libyan Desert. They were evacuated from there to Alexandria, and many of them were hospitalized at our Hospital or in comfortable Jewish homes, where they got individual warm and excellent care. They were now being brought to the French hospital in Ismailia, which belonged to the Suez Canal Society.

We finally arrived in Ismailia, and at our good friend's lodging. It consisted of one sparsely furnished room and an adjoining glass veranda, with three deck chairs. Herbert told us that Ismailia was overcrowded with a multitude of fleeing people and refugees, and that there was nothing available in town.

"Perhaps we can find some rooms at the Palace Hotel?" Mr. Rosenstein suggested, embarrassed that we should abuse the good man's charity.

"Believe me, there's no room or hole available in the

whole of Ismailia, and the Palace Hotel is entirely occupied by the British army," Herbert told us. "But don't worry, we'll manage fine here!" And we did.

We three young women occupied the three deck chairs on the veranda; the Rosensteins and their child occupied a corner in the corridor; Dr. Katz had one armchair in Herbert's room, and the chief manager of the Bata shoe shops had the other armchair. Every night, we managed to get some sleep, until the moment we heard again the familiar despicable roar coming nearer and becoming louder and louder. The German Spitfires spit their bombs and shells over our heads and into the Suez Canal almost every night. Most of these fell over the town itself, and there were many wounded. We were told that the anti-aircraft guns had been taken away from Ismailia for a strategic reason, and that all Ismailia had to rely on was *Allah*.

"God will surely protect its inhabitants," Ali, the old porter of the house, assured us, with a worried look that belied his words.

"*Inshallah*! May that be," I answered, but wished He could be helped by anti-aircraft guns in His difficult task...

Every evening before going to sleep, our friend told us not to wake him up if the alarm sirens rang only once, for then there was no danger to the ammunition depot. But if the sirens rang twice, we must wake him up immediately because then he had to run to the ammunition depot and set it afire before the enemy laid hands on it. Fortunately, we never had to wake him up. But sometimes he woke us up with his powerful snoring which sounded as if a giant kettle was boiling. We always wondered then if the noise we heard came from him, or if the enemy airplanes were again on their way to Ismailia.

We all had breakfast together, prepared by one of the women or the men. After that we sometimes went for a swim in the Bitter Lakes. We three young women made our way every morning to the railway station, to see if there was a train available. We had made friends with the railway staff, and they always had something important to tell us, as for instance, the good news about Rommel's army being at last forced to halt by Montgomery's troops at the Katara Depression, and about great quantities of war ammunitions coming through Ismailia. They also revealed to us that many Allied soldiers were concentrated there for a decisive attack soon. Their comforting words gave us courage, and I hoped with all my heart that they were right. We were also lucky from time to time to get a call through to the hospital. The few who stayed there gave us reassuring news, there were no more air attacks on Alexandria, and we took it as a good sign.

We had our lunches mostly at the Palace Hotel. We got there every day as soon as the luncheon room opened, as we didn't have much to do. It was very hot and humid in Ismailia, and we had nowhere to go to get away from the heat, except for one place: the Rex Cinema, which was the only one in town. As soon as it opened its doors, we bought our tickets and didn't move from our seats until the last performance was over. We saw during our eight-day stay the same picture three times a day. I remember it well, it was *Blood and Sand* with Rita Hayworth and Tyrone Power. These two fine actors skillfully sowed fictitious "blood and sand" before our eyes, which relieved our minds from the real tragedy and blood-shedding outside. After the first three performances, we didn't watch the screen anymore and fell asleep as soon as we came in, as it was difficult to get enough sleep on the veranda. The melodious accompanying music of the film was our lullaby.

At night when the last performance was over, we made our way home to the three deck chairs on the glass veranda and chatted the night away. We became still closer, as the bond of eminent danger gave greater meaning and a powerful impact to our friendship. We didn't complain about anything, neither the physical discomforts nor the anxiety in our souls, but tried to constantly keep our good humor. Every night there was a general blackout over all Ismailia. We were happy to have slept a little at the cinema and hoped that maybe that night the Spitfires wouldn't pay us a visit. But our hopes were always in vain. They came back every night and like demons from hell, they spit flames and shrieking bombs over our tired and anxious heads incessantly.

22

NURSES' PHANTOM TRAIN

On the sixth day when we went to the railway station, we were told that the day after, a train for civilians would leave Ismailia at eight o'clock in the morning for Alexandria. There hadn't been any civilian trains for a long time, and we were glad to hear there would be one. We had also received news by a South African ambulance driver that the front line at the Katara Depression was now safeguarded, and that there was almost no more danger of an invasion by the German Wehrmacht into Egypt. We were all overjoyed by the happy news and started making new plans. Six of us got permission to return to Alexandria by train and we bought six first-class tickets with the intention to occupy an entire compartment so that two of us at a time could lie down on the benches and sleep properly for the first time in eight days. We also did some shopping and bought instant coffee and filled our Thermos with hot water so that we could drink hot coffee on the way.

We arrived before seven o'clock at the railway station, and there indeed was our civilian train. We entered the first-class carriage and found to our dismay that every door was locked. The curtains were pulled over the windows, and there was a sinister silence. We went through all the carriages of the train, and it was the same thing everywhere, all the doors were locked, and all the windows were covered with curtains. We simply couldn't understand what kind of train this was! Was it a phantom train? Had we been duped?

We went out to the station manager and asked anxiously, "Where is the train to Alexandria?" He pointed to the ghost train.

"But it's all locked!" I cried in dismay.

"Yes, it's full of wounded passengers," he informed us. "They are British, American, Australian, and Canadian wounded nurses who have been saved from their wrecked hospital ship, which got hit last night by a German Spitfire. Sorry there are no seats for you, except perhaps some small folding chairs we can arrange for you in the corridor."

This sad information filled us with outrage and revulsion. I was deeply touched by the thought of these poor wounded nurses who themselves needed care, instead of being by the bedside of their patients that morning. In comparison, we were so lucky, we had been saved, and this feeling was mixed with guilt. Why should they suffer, while I was healthy and untouched? What was it that decided who would be saved and who wouldn't? For what reason? According to what criteria? Were there any reasons or criteria at all? Or was it all a game of chance? Why should God want to wound nurses who were so needed in this terrible war time? The questions came one after the other, in the order of a military phalanx. Each marched into my consciousness fully armed, was recognized, and proceeded to make way for the next.

My heart began to beat quicker. I felt more and more sorry for all those shipwrecked women who had been turned overnight by a treacherous Spitfire, from helping nurses into helpless patients. At our request the station manager opened the doors for us, and we offered our help to the poor nurses who were lying on the seats shivering under their blankets.

"Hot tea please, or hot coffee," they begged, while the train was just leaving Ismailia. We opened our thermos and prepared hot drinks as quickly as we could. Each one of the nurses got a cup of tea or coffee. At every stop, we got out of the train and asked for some hot water to fill our thermos, and gave more tea, coffee, pills, and sympathy to the nurses, who thanked us faintly. Finally, we arrived at the Alexandria railway station. Ambulances and hospital staff waited for the shipwrecked nurses. It was a sad sight to see them disembarking on stretchers that had been prepared for them. We helped them as much as we could and tried to boost their morale. They couldn't talk, but a few of them managed to give us a trembling handshake and half smiles of gratitude mingled with pain. On several of the pale faces streaked with tears, we could discern looks of incomprehension that such a tragedy had happened to them and that they had exchanged places with their patients.

Nobody was there to receive us, as we hadn't notified

the hospital that we would arrive. We silently took a taxi and made our own way to the hospital. There was a special excitement about our return, and we were relieved to be back home. Ismailia under the awful atmosphere of the Spitfires had been an exhausting and nerve wracking experience.

"I told you, you would soon come back, Schwester Thea," Mohammed said with a bright twinkle in his eyes. "You drank Nile water before you went, didn't you? So, you just had to come back!" I smiled gratefully at his happiness in seeing us back safe and sound, and especially at his friendship.

We were exhausted and went to sleep straight away. The next morning, we started our daily work promptly on time, as we had always done before our departure to Ismailia, just as if nothing had happened. We were so happy to be safely back and working again, we felt this was our own small victory over Hitler's army. They had not succeeded to trap, harm or disable us. It gave us a secret source of strength to try to create a still more attractive and caring attitude in the Hospital and in our world.

When Rommel and his army were at length forced to a standstill at El Alamein, the whole area from Alexandria to El Alamein became a vast military camp. There were no bombings of Alexandria anymore, but the Allies were preparing their counter-attack. The night it started we heard terrible roaring and shrieking again, not the same kind though, it was longer, more sonorous, and further away. We went up to the roof of the hospital again, and from there we saw in the far distance enormous blazing fireballs. They lit the whole skies with fiery orange and green and were not extinguished for several days and nights. The Allies' victorious battle had begun. We looked and rejoiced, with tears in our hearts and smiles in our eyes. The wounding of the poor disabled nurses, soldiers and civilians was being paid for. What was left of Rommel's army retreated in fear through the Libyan Desert, never to be seen in these parts again.

23

THE ASTOUNDING
PANCHO EPISODE

One afternoon a huge crowd of visitors was waiting at the gate of the hospital to be let in to visit their relatives and friends. Among the crowd was a port policeman. He asked the gatekeeper for the doctor, and was told to go to the first floor. The doctor was not available and the policeman was sent to me.

"There are four sick people in the port prison, Schwester," he said. "They are Jews, and are very sick. Maybe you could hospitalize them here. The physician in charge of the port prisoners gave me permission to ask for your help. These four men have been in prison for two days, and their state is worsening dangerously. Please come quickly, Schwester."

We both rushed to the port prison in my tiny Morris Minor. There I found four very sick and miserable young men in a room, together with ten Chinese sailors. The prison doctor was informed about my arrival, he came promptly and having examined the four young men, agreed that they should be hospitalized, but on one usual condition--a police guard should be stationed at each of their bedsides. We accepted his condition, and we ordered an ambulance for the four patients. I called the Internal Department of the hospital to prepare four beds, and warmly thanked the prison doctor and the kind guard for their collaboration. The ambulance came and our new patients went to sleep in comfortable beds for the first time after their dangerous sea voyage. The four policemen arrived shortly after and took their seats beside the beds of their prisoners. It took a few days until we finally learned the details of their story.

It began in Czechoslovakia in 1941. They belonged to a group of three hundred Jews from Czechoslovakia who escaped during the Hitler invasion and had chartered a ship by the name of *Pancho*, in Constanza, with the intention of sailing to Palestine. Sailing there was illegal, because none of them was in possession of an entry visa to Palestine. They had a dreadful time trying to avoid warships in the Mediterranean Sea, and they sailed without a flag. Their ship was overcrowded and very old, and after a few days of sailing it completely broke down. An emergency debarkation had to be made, on an uninhabited island, probably not far from Crete or Cyprus. They abandoned the ship just in time. When the last dinghy full of people was lowered, the ship heaved its last sigh with a tremendous noise, and sank to the bottom of the sea. Unfortunately, and to their great dismay, they found out that there was no water or food on the desert island. The refugees soon realized, with sinking hearts, that without outside help they would not last long. When everybody was ashore on the island, these four young men decided to try to get to Crete, Cyprus or Rhodes and ask for help there. They found a small old broken cutter on the beach, repaired it, put a white piece of material on a stick as a flag, and took to the sea with the hope of reaching help.

On the second day of their voyage they suddenly saw an airplane coming down and circling around their cutter. They rapidly waved the white flag, but the plane disappeared in the far distance. The four men were starved, exhausted, and afraid of drowning in the stormy sea. At one point, they saw two big sharks dangerously sniffing their little boat, but they luckily disappeared. On the second day, they were so tired and weak that they could not handle the cutter anymore. They decided not to sail any further, and to just wait for a miracle. A few hours later they were surrounded by British warships on all sides. A destroyer approached the cutter, and a cord ladder was thrown into it. A sailor on the destroyer shouted and gesticulated that they should come aboard the warship. It was not such an easy operation, as they had no strength left, but they finally managed to do so and were promptly surrounded by several British sailors. They were taken to the captain, and declared prisoners of war. The four young men talked in German as they only knew a few words of English. They argued that they were not German though, and that their documents proved that they were Czechoslovakian citizens, and were Jewish fugitives fleeing from the Nazis.

One of the young men, named Joseph, even showed him the silver *Magen David* he wore on a chain around his neck. But it was all in vain. The captain was convinced that they were German spies, and had false documents.

"Yes, yes, we heard all about you spies, trying to get aboard our warships. Those darned Germans they even provided you with a Jewish *Magen David*! We will send you straight to prison at the next port, and no use arguing." Fortunately, the destroyer's next destination was the port of Alexandria, where they finally arrived and were handed over to the Egyptian port authorities, who put them in prison. When their condition worsened the next day, the good-hearted Egyptian policeman decided to come to our hospital for help and to inform us about the plight of these four Jews.

During their delirium, the four young men whispered all the time: "Save them, please save them!" But we couldn't get more details out of them on that first day they were hospitalized. On the second day, Joseph recovered enough to be able to tell us the tragic story about their stranded families and friends in danger of starvation on the uninhabited island. It was painful to watch the twitching mouths of the three friends who followed his story whispering ominously all the while, "Water, water, or they'll die! The three hundred of them--they'll all perish!" The depth of agony in their eyes was unbearable.

We tried everything in order to save the stranded refugees on their barren, unknown Mediterranean island. I ran to the British authorities in Alexandria, who were aghast on hearing this tragic episode, and they promised they would send a plane at once to that region to find the stranded fugitives and to arrange for their rescue. But they reported that they did not discover anything. Did they really look for them? I am not sure about that to this day.

It took a few weeks until the four young men recovered completely. They worried all the time about the fate of their relatives and friends they had left behind on the barren island, when they went to seek help. Finally, we had to discuss the future of these four refugees. What could be done for them? What were their plans? They told me they had decided to fight with the Allies against Hitler. They considered this to be their main task in life now, and the best way to avenge themselves for what had happened to their families and friends. They wanted to be incorporated either into the Czechoslovakian exile army or into the British army. But none of them was in possession of even one single document, because all their papers had been confiscated by the commander of the destroyer. What could we do? How could they get some kind of identity card, and from which authority? Whom could we ask for advice?

I decided to bring the case before the British vice consul in Alexandria, whom I knew personally, as he had been a patient at our hospital and was very kind and appreciative of his treatment. He was Maltese, but a British subject. Many Maltese people, especially those working for the Alexandria traffic police, had been treated at our hospital. In addition, we had hospitalized several Maltese civilians when the German Luftwaffe had bombed Malta and wounded many people. These civilians had been airlifted from Malta by the British

Royal Air Force to Alexandria and they were brought to our hospital. They were all very grateful to us for our charitable services, and for saving so many of their lives.

I went to the British consulate and reported the misadventure of the four unfortunate young men to the vice-consul and conveyed their wish to enter either the Czechoslovakian or the British army. He listened to me solemnly without interrupting. When I finished relating my story, he burst out, "This is unbelievable! Come with me to a certain person and retell your story."

I followed him through a long whitewashed, narrow corridor, which reminded me of those in Joseph Kafka's books. However, this story has a quite different end than in Kafka's stories. We entered a room and behind a large desk sat a neat, prim Englishman in civilian clothes. Later I found out he was the liaison officer between the British army and the Czechoslovakian army. He took my name and address and asked me about my nurse's uniform. I told him I was the head nurse at the Jewish Hospital. I was invited to sit down and to repeat my story and the request of the four men.

He listened, took a few notes, and then stood up. "We shall consider the request, and you will soon get an answer," he said politely and I could detect a note of empathy in his tone.

A few days later a red-haired Englishman in civilian clothes came and asked to interview the four Jews. I accompanied him and had to translate for them, because their English was very poor.

"Are you still interested in joining the army?" he questioned them. And when they assured him they did, he asked further, "Have you ever been in the Czechoslovakian army?"

None of them had served in any army yet. They had been too young to join. He shook their hands and said good-bye. They would get an answer soon. After some time, the same red-haired Englishman came again to meet the young men and told them that they had been admitted into the Czecho-slovakian exile army in Egypt, which was affiliated to the Allied troops. Documents had to be signed, and they each received an identity card. A few days later a Czech official came to take charge of them.

The whole hospital staff took part in the farewell party we prepared for them. We had all become very attached to them, and everyone hugged them and wished them all the best. The four young men started their military careers as soldiers in El Alamein, chasing the Rommel army out of the Libyan Desert. Then they were sent to Italy, where they fought at Monte Casino. From there they were sent to England, and then back again to Europe for the great invasion at Normandy which ended the Second World War and brought down Hitler's Nazi regime.

Finally, the four young men could return to their homeland. They searched for their families everywhere in Czechoslovakia and unfortunately found only one person left; the rest of all their families who had remained at home had been deported to the extermination camps. They searched for signs of the *Pancho* fugitives but there were none. It was as if they had been swallowed by the waves. A meticulous search of all the probable islands in that region, did not reveal any signs of any human bones. Three of the four men emigrated to Palestine, where they got married and built families of their own; the fourth one traveled to South America.

One of those who settled in Israel is Imi Lichtenfeld, became the director of gymnastic activities at the Wingate Institute, near Natanya. He is well-known for his special self-defense method which he developed with great success. He is appreciated by all, and we have kept in touch to this day. But for half a century we did not find out what became of the poor *Pancho* fugitives who had completely disappeared as if into thin air.

24

MYSTERIOUS RESCUE

Only half a century later did we find out at last what had become of the three hundred poor Czechoslovakians stranded on that barren and hostile island in the Mediterranean with no provisions whatsoever. The writer, Ada Aharoni, who was writing my biography and researched this episode, had just published an article in The Jerusalem Post, in memory of the astounding *Pancho* episode and the mysterious disappearance half a century before of its three hundred destitute passengers. Soon after, a breathless man called her from New York and reported, "I have just read your article Dr. Aharoni, and am so excited! I am from the *Pancho*! Would you like to hear what happened to us after the four young men sailed away to seek help?"

Ada was speechless for a few minutes, as it seemed to her that a ghost from the land of the dead was on the other side of the line. "After the three young men sailed away," the man from New York, whose name was Abraham, reported, "an Italian warship spotted us and the Captain came ashore with part of his crew to find out who we were. He was deeply moved by our story and by the sobs of our children who were so hungry and thirsty. This kind-hearted Captain, whose name was Carlo, decided to take us all aboard and he gave instructions to the sailors to feed and clothe us. We thanked him warmly, but were afraid that he might hand us to the Germans, who would have surely sent us to the death camps.

The next day Captain Carlo called Abraham and a delegation of Czechoslovakians to his cabin, and he informed them that he had decided to take them to Sicily, though it meant changing his course and disobeying his orders. "But I can't leave you with all your cute *bambinos* to die, can I? If I do so, you'll be on my conscience all my life!"

"But how will we manage in Sicily?" Abraham asked.

"We will teach you some Italian, until we get there. Don't say you're Jews, just tell them you are fugitives from the North, and you'll be able to stay there until this mad war is over!"

"Captain Carlo was as good as his word," Abraham related. "He himself taught a group of fugitives some useful Italian words, and he organized the sailors to teach other groups. We learned quickly, but still had great fear in our hearts that the Sicilian *Fascists*, members of Mussolini's party, would discover who we really were, and would deliver us to the authorities. But none of this happened. We lived and worked in Sicily until the end of the war, and nobody harmed us."

If you think this is the end of the story then you're wrong.

Several of these strange tales I've related, have mysteriously acquired a life and a momentum of their own as has this astounding *Pancho* episode.

After the publication of the article, Ada Aharoni was invited to talk about her books and her research, in Torino in Italy. When she was speaking about the *Pancho* episode, she related how that kind Captain Carlo saved the life of the three hundred Czechoslovakian Jews by taking them to Sicily, even though it was in the middle of the war. Suddenly a tall, stalwart man with a smart Navy-blue cap, and a profuse gray beard and mustache, stood up, and stated in a deep voice: "But I didn't take them to Sicily, I took them to my hometown, to Calabria, they must have gone to Sicily later on." There was dead silence in the hall, while Ada and all the audience looked at him in surprise and joy. She called him to the platform, and he related several details she had not known. She thanked him and shook his hand gratefully, as well as many people in the audience. Abraham and I have since been in touch with Captain Carlo, who had proved to be a real humanist, half a century before.

However, the finest thing which came out of the article, is that a Czechoslovakian family from the *Pancho*, that was living in New York, found their long-lost son in Jerusalem! The family did not know that the four young men had survived, and they were sure that they had drowned in the stormy sea or had been eaten by sharks. Their joy knew no bounds on finding their son alive and well. In gratitude to Providence for having brought their son back from the dead, they organized a *Pancho* reunion in Jerusalem in

1990, of all the families who had been saved. I was invited to that moving historic and memorable reunion to which the former fugitives came from all the five continents, including Australia and South America. I will never forget the shining faces and the cries of joy people emitted when they recognized and hugged each other after half a century. Captain Carlo was invited to the reunion too, and to the warm homes of the people he saved. Watching the humane and brave Captain Carlo, I mused, Hitler and Mussolini are long dead, but the kindness and benevolence of Carlo's action lives on, and will continue flourishing in the minds and hearts of all these grateful people, as well as in readers'.

25

SPY

The war continued, and we couldn't see its end. The German citizens who hadn't left Egypt were gradually interned in concentration camps outside Alexandria, as well as the men of the large Italian community in Alexandria and Cairo. Both German and Italian citizens were classified as enemy aliens, as Egypt was ruled by the British High Commissioner. Rumors were spreading throughout the town of Alexandria that the Germans and Italians were signaling every night, with the help of searchlights, to the German and Italian air forces and indicating targets in Alexandria. Both air forces came back every night and continued throwing bombs over the town, and especially over the port area.

Unfortunately, the small German-Jewish community was ridiculously also considered enemy aliens. The governorate, the Egyptian *Mohafza*, issued us red, enemy identity cards with a big "J" (Jew) on it, and we always had to ask for a special permit to leave the town of Alexandria. But we always got the permit without any difficulty. At the beginning, nothing changed in our way of life at the hospital, and each of us continued doing his or her daily duties. In the meantime, correspondence with our relatives in Germany had come to a complete stop since the outbreak of the war. We were deeply worried about our families, and wondered what we could do to help them, in addition to our previous efforts and our constant pleading with the British authorities.

One day at two o'clock a.m. I heard a loud knock at my door. The physician on duty told me to get dressed quickly and come up immediately to the Operations Ward, where three Egyptian policemen and two English security men were waiting.

"Please open the room of Dr. Fritz Katz, the chief surgeon," they ordered.

"Before I do this, I want to know why and to get in touch with him," I said politely.

"You cannot do that," the senior officer informed me coldly.

"His apartment has been searched already, and he himself has been arrested and deported to a concentration camp near Cairo."

I was shocked. "Dr. Katz?" I cried. "Impossible! But why?"

"He is suspected of being a German spy." the officer answered curtly.

"This is a ridiculous witch-hunt! It can only be a false accusation," I protested. "Dr. Katz is only interested in medicine and in his own work here at the hospital. You're making a great mistake and have to release him immediately!"

However, all my entreaties fell on deaf ears, and I had to open the door of his room. They ordered me to leave them alone and to go down to my room in the Nurses' Compound, because it would soon also be searched, for I too was suspected of being a German spy! I couldn't believe my ears, and I went down to my room, tears burning my eyes, and my throat constricting as if I had swallowed forceps.

Two policemen and a security man, went back with me to my room. John, the security man, I knew well; he was a Maltese who had been hospitalized at our Hospital in the past, and he had told us then that he was in charge of the Narcotics Department for the Alexandrian police. I asked the three men not to raise their voices in order not to wake the nurses. The policemen stood outside, and the security man entered my small room.

"But this is ridiculous John," I told him, "you know me well. How can I, a Jew, be a German spy? How can Dr. Katz, who is so loved and venerated by all his patients and who spends all of his hours in the operating room, be a spy?"

"I'm just obeying orders, Sister Thea," John said uneasily, not daring to look into my eyes.

About an hour later the Egyptian policemen and the second security man came into my room too, and started the search. They turned the whole room upside down and even opened the mattress! I don't know to this day what they expected to find there.

"But I'm Jewish!" I cried. "I would never help the Nazis!"

My protests and frantic explanations fell on deaf ears. Jewish or not Jewish did not matter to them. In their eyes, I was first of all a German.

Regina, the head nurse of the Surgical Ward for men, woke up from the noise, put on her nightgown, and came to find out what was happening. She quickly took in what was going on. She pursed her mouth, turned around, and came back after a few minutes with a cup of Turkish coffee for me. It warmed my heart and stomach, and helped me to get a hold of myself. She waited at the door until I had sipped it, left again, and prepared another cup of coffee for John, though he didn't merit it at all. She repeated this a few times until the moment she overhead that I had to accompany the police to the police station. It was already 5:30 in the morning. Nearly all the nurses had woken up by then, and they came to see what was going on in my room.

"Don't get excited," I told them. "My room has been searched, and Dr. Katz has been arrested under the pretense that he is a German spy. And now they want to take me also to the police station. The nurses were aghast; they couldn't believe their ears. They tried to argue with the policemen, but it was to no avail.

"Please inform the director of the hospital, Mr. Benvenisti, and the head of the Jewish community, Mr. Toriel, and also all the medical staff," I told them, trying to keep my voice cool, "and most of all, business as usual." I tried to be as composed as I could, but my heart was heavy, and my head swam. I hoped it was just a horrible nightmare and that I would soon wake up.

I then turned to John. "I refuse to come with you!" I said point-blank, trying to make my voice sound firm and determined.

"But you must, Sister Thea," he insisted. "Please don't cause trouble. I'm just doing my duty," he repeated automatically, his voice sounding like a scratched, burlesque comedy record.

"First of all, I'm *not* a German spy," I argued, "secondly, a nurse possesses immunity. She can never be taken into custody!" I started to shout and cry, and threw myself onto the ground, as if I had a fit. The nurses ran with cognac and poured it into my mouth. I took the bottle and spilled it all over John. "This is my answer!" I shouted. "Now go and look for real German spies!" He was very surprised and didn't know what to do.

Suddenly Princess Amina Toussoun, a close relative of King Farouk's, who worked as a volunteer nurse in our operating ward, appeared. Nurse Regina, in her quiet way, had given the alarm.

"What's happening here?" Princess Toussoun cried. "How dare you treat Schwester Thea in this way? I'm going to call the High Commissioner over the phone and tell him what's going on here!" She went out and came back after some time; I was still lying down on the floor, shouting and crying. She told the police to leave the Nurses' Compound immediately, but without me. Her tone was majestic, and they obeyed the princess's order immediately.

"But please promise, Sister Thea, that you will not leave the hospital premises," Captain John begged.

"I'm on duty for the whole day," I said. "I shall start doing my daily job, but I don't give any promises to anybody, and especially not to you!" The nurses patted my back proudly, and Amina smiled at me in approval.

All the five of them left with open mouths and empty hands. They of course couldn't find anything suspicious to take away, neither in my room nor in Dr. Katz's room, and were peevish and apologetic when Sister Regina accompanied them to the door. They even thanked her for her hot coffee.

It didn't take long until the whole town knew what had happened during the night, and about the arrest of the chief surgeon, Dr. Katz. There was a continuous going and coming of people asking what they could do to help us. I gave them all the same answer, "You have to get Dr. Katz out of the prison as quickly as possible!" It took us two weeks to free him. The day he returned, he immediately went back to work on the operating table. When we asked him about his imprisonment, he pursed his lips and refused to share his experience or thoughts about his internment with anybody.

He had been interned in a concentration camp in Cairo where the gentile Germans were interned; but luckily, he had his own room. During all this time, visits were not allowed. We were only informed that on such and such a day he would be freed. We never knew the whole story, and by what means he was liberated. There was some whispering about a war correspondent named Wallace, who worked for an influential American newspaper, who had helped. He had interviewed the high British commander in Cairo, about Dr. Katz' arrest and voiced his outrage that the commander could allow such a kind of thing. The British were very much interested then in a favorable report concerning British war efforts, and especially, in influencing the United States to declare war on the Germans.

After the interview, good friends of the chief surgeon gave a warm farewell party to Wallace, the war correspondent, and also invited the British general there. The general thanked the American journalist for his thorough interview, and asked him: "Can I do anything for you?"

"Yes, certainly," Wallace answered unhesitatingly, "Please liberate Dr. Katz, because he is not a German spy; he is a Jewish refugee and only interested in healing the sick." The next day Dr. Katz was liberated.

26

GUSTAV

I remember a painful event concerning the signaling by torchlights. There was a well-known family in town by the name of Levy. They had two daughters, Sarina, the plain older sister who couldn't find a husband, and Lina, the pretty, slim and mischievous one who played the piano so well and who had many suitors. She chose one of them, by the name of Gaby, but at the beginning, her parents would not allow her to get married until her elder sister, Sarina, got married. At length Lina was allowed to get married, but poor Sarina was in danger of becoming a spinster, and her parents were very worried about her.

Then suddenly a miracle happened, Sarina became engaged, then married, to a tall handsome, mysterious young man, a refugee from Bavaria, by the name of Gustav. She had met him at a N.A.F.I. music concert which she never missed as she liked classical music very much. Sarina and Gustav had instantly fallen in love with each other, and decided to get married. We were all invited to the beautiful wedding at the Synagogue, and it was with a great joy to see the happiness on Sarina's face as well as her parents'. The wedding included many paragons of urban elegance, from Cairo and Alexandria. Gustav smiled his secretive half-smile and stood up handsome and tall. Where are his guests, I wondered, as everybody else did? Doesn't he have any family or friends at all? Nobody seemed to be able to enlighten us on that point. Gustav did not like to be questioned, and we supposed he did not want to be reminded of his relatives left behind in Nazi Germany.

A year later a beautiful baby girl was born, and they named her Marguerite. She had her father's large, deep-set blue eyes, and his fine bone structure and her mother's brown, curly hair. She was a healthy and energetic baby and we all took to her.

Then the calamity happened. One day we heard that Gustav had been arrested by the police as a German spy. I could hardly believe the news and ran to buy a copy of *Le Journal d'Egypte*. "This must be another witch-hunt of imaginary spies" I thought, "just like when they arrested Dr. Katz and wanted to arrest me!" I hurriedly read all the details and found out to my dismay that Gustav had been caught by the police signaling with a torchlight from the roof of his house. He had been handed at once to the British Intelligence Service, who investigated him thoroughly, and then deported him to Malta. The paper related that he had married a Jewish girl on purpose so that he would have a good cover; he had probably received orders to do so. He chose to live in the port area where he could carry on his spying unmolested, and Sarina, who was reluctant to refuse her beloved Gustav anything, accepted, though it was dangerous to live near the port then, as it was often attacked my German and Italian war planes. She loved Gustav, and did not suspect anything.

After he was arrested, Sarina never saw him again. The poor girl became very sick after the news spread that he was a real Nazi spy, and not like Dr. Katz. Sarina was brought to our hospital, and she was under severe shock for a long time. Her parents and sister took care of Marguerite all the while and often brought her to the Hospital to see her mother. When she became better, I asked Sarina one night if she had ever noticed anything peculiar about Gustav during the year she had been married to him.

"Yes, he was peculiar in many ways," she said quietly. "He was so distant, silent, and secretive... and I never really understood what his work was about."

"But didn't you notice the signaling?" I queried.

She hesitated then said, "From the first week of our marriage, he started waking up in the middle of the night, and when I inquired what the matter was, he told me not to worry, that he had developed a kidney infection and had to go to the bathroom often. I wondered why he went up to the roof, or opened the balcony every time he did--but now I know why!" and she burst out crying. I consoled her, and she continued, "In addition, he had those two locked suitcases in his wardrobe, which he was obsessed with, and did not allow anybody to touch. When I asked him what they contained he impatiently answered that they contained special samples of precious materials he did not want me and the maid to handle. "As an expert textile merchant, my samples have to be perfect if I want to sell them," he added ruefully. I saw how disturbed he was and never questioned him again about his samples.

It was hard for Sarina to recover from the shock that her beloved Marguerite was the daughter of a Nazi spy. We tried to help her as much as we could, but the scar was too deep and too fresh in her memory. Her last question to me was: "I wonder if Gustav loved me at all?"

Sarina and her daughter are both in Paris today, where Marguerite has married, and has two beautiful children of her own. They both have their grandfather's deep-set, blue eyes and his sharp mind. Yet, to this day, neither Marguerite nor her children,[6] know the true story of Gustav.

6   The names in this story, as in some of the others have been changed, so as not to cause further unnecessary pain

27

STARVING FUGITIVES AND AISHA THE HADJA

The summer of 1945 was a hot and humid one. World War Two was just over, and joy was in our hearts, but it also included much pain. It was midday rest for the patients, and also for some of the nurses. Suddenly there was a knock at my door, and one of our Muslim nurses, Massouda, asked me to come up to the ward quickly, because a policeman from the main railroad station wanted to talk to me urgently.

The policeman told me the following story: A train full of men, women, and children had earlier arrived from the port railway station to the main railway station. "The people on it are Jews," he said, "who arrived the day before on a huge British ship from Greece. A few British soldiers are in charge of the train, which is to leave in a few hours for Palestine. These poor people haven't had any food or drink for more than two days, and don't have any either for their trip to Palestine. They are thirsty, starving, and penniless and some of them will surely die if we don't help them. Can you please help them, Sister Thea?" he asked pleadingly, his eyes dimming while he spoke.

"Of course," I said unhesitatingly.

"We must hurry, because the train is due to leave the railway station soon," the policeman urged me.

"How many are they?" I asked.

"There seems to be hundreds of them," he answered, fidgeting impatiently. I thanked the kind-hearted *shaouish* (policeman) warmly, and gave orders that food should be prepared for the refugees on the train as quickly as possible.

With the help of several nurses and kitchen assistants, we started to prepare cheese and egg sandwiches, which we got from the hospital kitchen. Massouda was sent out to buy soft drinks, chocolate, lollipops and toilet paper. Pills for headaches we got from our main pharmacy and we collected cups from the staff room. Kind Aisha, in charge of our laundry department, lent us some big laundry baskets, and we hurriedly put all the food in it. In no more than half an hour everything was ready.

Massouda, two other nurses and I, drove to the railway station quickly. There we found the train on the tracks to Lydda. Some British soldiers were patrolling around, making sure that no one left the train. They were surprised when they saw us arriving with the laundry baskets and asked us the reason for our coming, which we promptly explained. The poor refugees were hanging out over the open windows, and signs of terrible distress and thirst were on their faces. We started immediately to distribute the victuals we had brought with us. They couldn't believe their eyes; they thanked us joyfully, and ate and drank ravenously. Most of them were revived, and only a few still lay down on the benches motionless.

"But who are you?" the astonished passengers asked in surprise.

One of the young travelers, a handsome young man with a mustache, said, "Can't you see who they are? It's clear, they're charming guardian angels sent to us by God!"

I laughed. "Not guardian angels, just ordinary Jewish and Arab nurses from the Jewish Hospital in Alexandria."

Many of the passengers looked up at us in amazement.

"Jewish Hospital in Egypt?" a man with a blue beret asked. "I didn't, on my life, even know that there were still Jews in Egypt! Didn't they all leave during the Biblical Exodus?" His bright green eyes looked at us in utter astonishment.

"Most of them did," I said smiling, "but two thousand and six hundred years ago, after the destruction of the First Temple, the prophet Jeremiah and his followers came to Egypt, and since then there has always been a Jewish community in Egypt." The man nodded in amazement, whistling softly.

"May I please touch your hand, to make sure you're not an angel?" an elderly woman asked. I gave her my hand, and she kept it for quite a while, with tears in her eyes. She began to tell us about their painful odyssey.

"Finally escaping from the horrors of Nazi Europe, we were stranded in Greece," she said, "put there in a concentration camp again, after all the atrocities we went through in the

Nazi concentration camps, and then liberated by the British when they conquered Greece. Then we were embarked in Piraeus on a British warship and brought to the port of Alexandria. From there we were put in this train this morning where we thought we would die of thirst and hunger before reaching Palestine. Since our transfer to the train we have been without any food or drink, and if it were not for you, many of us would have fainted or died soon. God bless you Schwester."

All the rest of the food was distributed and quickly consumed, and the train started to move. We shook as many hands as we could, while tears ran down cheeks, and handkerchiefs came out and fluttered warm good-byes and thanks from every window of every train carriage. We were deeply moved by their warm gratitude, and contented that we had been of help. Another train was already coming in, and passengers looked at us and at our empty baskets curiously. After thanking the good-natured policeman warmly, we left the station and drove back to the hospital. We couldn't believe what had happened between one o'clock and four o'clock. The whole episode was a swift and dramatic as a dream. But it had a strange and fruitful outcome. Coming back to the hospital, we returned the baskets to Aisha at the laundry, and to the kind Arab women who had helped us prepare the food. Aisha wanted to know the purpose of this urgent request for food and for her baskets, and we told her the whole story, which moved her to tears.

A few days later Aisha came to me. "In the dream I dreamed last night," she said, "I saw all these destitute Jewish people on the train, and in order to protect them on their way, I have decided to make a pilgrimage to Mecca. Would you be willing to help me finance it?" she queried wistfully.

"I'll ask the hospital board," I said, taken aback by her strange request.

We discussed her request among us, and with the board, and I was happy to bring her our decision: "Yes, we are willing." Before she left for Mecca she was surrounded by many well-wishers with wide smiles and loud congratulations.

Aisha made her pilgrimage to Mecca with our financial help and returned from there as a *hadja*, a holy woman. When she came back she related proudly, "I told everybody who asked me for the purpose of my pilgrimage, the real reason for it; the laundry baskets I had given to be filled with bread and drink for the poor refugees who were dying of hunger, who were *Yehudi* and destitute, because of that monster Hitler, may he rot in Hell!" I hugged the new "hadja" warmly, and the human bond between us became still deeper; extending beyond all religions and spreading large baskets full of love and fortitude.

This is another of those stories which does not end here, but has a surprising sequence many years later. In the year 1963, seventeen years after the train episode, I was for a short time in charge of an office for restitution to German Jewish refugees in New York. One morning I interviewed a couple and had to find out some details concerning their whereabouts on a specific date in the year 1945.

The husband looked at his wife, and after a while he said

to me, "I suppose you wouldn't believe what I am telling you now, but it's the truth. On this specific date, my wife and I were stationed in a train in Alexandria's main railway station in Egypt. We were brought there by the British, and unfortunately, left to starve there for two days. I don't have any proof of this, but I remember three charming nurses from the Jewish Hospital in Alexandria who suddenly appeared from nowhere and distributed sandwiches, drinks and money among us, just an hour before the train had to leave for Palestine. Maybe there is still a Jewish nurse at the hospital in Alexandria who remembers this."

I looked at the couple in amazement. "Yes, I remember very well, because I was one of the nurses who came to the station!"

They couldn't believe that at first, but in comparing some of the details, the whole adventure was vividly recreated in our minds. They told me, among other things, that they had all wondered how we had heard about them. "Who informed you about us being so hungry and thirsty at the railway station? Was it the British?" the man queried.

Then I told them about the kind-hearted Egyptian policeman who had taken pity on them and had come to the hospital for help, through his own initiative. They were surprised and pleased. "So, there were more than three angel-nurses involved," the man smiled quietly. "There was also a *shaouish*-policeman angel!" We all laughed heartily.

"What happened to you when you left Alexandria?" I asked.

"We arrived in Lydda and were put again in a camp by

the British for some time," the woman related. "But we finally got an affidavit from our children who lived in New York, and at length arrived where we originally wanted to be--in the United States, near our children."

"But we never forgot the charming guardian angels who appeared in our starving train," the husband added, and shook my hand warmly. The three of us had tears in our eyes and wonder in our hearts at the extraordinary and mysterious ways of Providence.

28

FROM MAURITIUS TO THE SINAI DESERT

At the end of July 1945, I found one morning among my mail a letter from Albert Mosseri, who worked for UNRWA, addressed to the "Committee for Jewish Refugees." It contained a request of aid for sixty-four Jewish refugees living in the El-Shatt UNRWA camps in the Sinai Desert, among 20,000 European refugees, most of them from Yugoslavia. These people were deported at the outbreak of World War Two by the British authorities to the island of Mauritius, when they tried to leave Austria and reach Palestine. They were now in transition in El-Shatt waiting to be repatriated, and were destitute and in urgent need of everything. I have kept a copy of the letter for almost forty years and have always wondered why. Now I know why.

Mr. Albert Mosseri, UNRWA/DID
El Shatt Camps, M.E.F.
Dr. Fritz Katz and Sister Thea Wolf
Committee for Jewish Refugees from Europe
The Jewish Hospital in Alexandria

July 30, 1945

Dear Dr. Katz and Sister Thea,

I am writing to thank you again for your constant
and generous help to our destitute refugees from
Europe.

We have just received in El-Shatt Camp, in the
Sinai Desert, a new group of 64 Jewish refugees,
whose names I include in the attached list. These
people are in a desperate state, and practically
need everything. They have just arrived from the
Isle of Mauritius, and are weak and helpless, and
there are many sick people amongst them. They
ran away from Europe five years ago, and have
since been kept in camps. As you can imagine,
many of them did not survive.

These poor people need literally everything,
starting from money and medicine to food and
warm clothes for the approaching winter. The
stories they related to me about their various
escapes from the Nazi Regime are blood-curdling,
and have brought bitter tears to my eyes. I feel

so helpless, for as you know, our budget here is ridiculously small. However, in thinking about you and your kind help in the past, I have regained strength and hope. I feel confident that you will again be able to convince the Board of the Jewish Community in Egypt to help us again now, as they have so often done in the past.

I beg you to do your utmost to alleviate the plight of these unfortunate refugees from Nazi Europe, who have been victimized again and again with no reason, except that they are Jewish. I am sure that you will again be sensitive to so much pain and need.

In the hope that I will soon receive a favorable answer, I send you dear Doctor Katz and dear Sister Thea, my very best wishes and salutations.

Sincerely,
Albert Mosseri

I answered immediately, telling him to ask the refugees to send us a specific list of their requests. I promised Mr. Mosseri that as soon as we got these details, we would do our utmost to fulfill their requests and to deliver the stuff they needed to them personally. We received sixty-four requests and learned that many of the refugees were elderly people. Most of them had caught malaria in Mauritius because of the damp climate and the conditions under which they had had to live during their long imprisonment in the camps. In addition to their basic needs for medicine, food and clothes, there were specific requests from individuals, as for instance: a paralyzed man asked for a wheelchair, another one for a straw hat, a woman for a corset, a young girl for a brassiere, and three people for spectacles. They also asked for coffee, soap, winter coats, shoes, warm slippers, and many other items. We copied the requests of the sixty-four people, sent them to the Jewish board and our friends in Alexandria, and asked them to please comply as quickly as possible to the wishes of these unfortunate refugees. Their response was overwhelming, and we were moved by their promptness and extreme generosity.

In the meantime, Dr. Lessing, a German refugee, and I, who had both decided to make the trip to El-Shatt, needed a permit from the Egyptian frontier authorities in Cairo in order to cross the Suez Canal into the Sinai Desert. We eventually got the permit without too much difficulty. We received many more clothes and other items than we had asked for. We prepared sixty-four parcels and decided that the surplus would be donated to the UNRWA authorities at the camp.

We had to rent a large truck that could contain all the stuff. We found a truck owner who agreed to drive the goods and us from Alexandria to Port Taufiq, which was quite a long distance. He also agreed to stay overnight in a hotel in Port Taufiq, drive the truck to the ferry station at the Suez Canal--where it would board the ferry across the canal--and then drive it to the El-Shatt UNRWA camp in the desert. The departure was fixed to be two days before Yom Kippur, 1945. The refugees were informed about our arrival, and in their reply, they explained to us that there was only one road leading from the ferry station to the camp, and that we would surely recognize it by its multitude of tents in an otherwise empty desert. And so, on the day set we left Alexandria, drove to Port Taufiq and stayed there overnight as planned, at the only hotel there. Early the next morning the ferry with the large truck on it crossed the canal and drove us to the road leading to the El-Shatt camp.

Ali, our Egyptian driver, was neither tired nor thirsty, but he was extremely worried, and he asked us again and again where we were taking him to in the middle of nowhere, where there was no sign of life, and where only the *Afrit*, devil, lived. This sinister trip was a dangerous enigma to him, and he was afraid that we were leading him astray in a forbidden land of ghosts and devils.

We reassured him, "There are people living in this desert who are in need of the stuff you have on your truck." And he looked doubtfully upwards toward heaven and asked Allah for protection for himself and for us.

"This journey is very dangerous," he said fearfully. "You are strangers and do not know about the *Afrit* (devil), in these isolated parts, but he will surely turn up soon if we don't turn back...."

We finally spotted the tents in the far distance and pointed them out to him joyfully. We drove faster to make sure that it was not a mirage. Ali suddenly stopped the truck, came out and kneeled down in the hot sand, thanking Allah for bringing us safely to where there were signs of life again, and where the *Afrit* will not dare appear.

We arrived at the gate of the camp about noon and showed our permits to the South African guards there. The barrier went up and we entered an enormous camp. On the way, we saw a pretty blond girl and asked her how we could find either the administration building or the Goldberger family.

"I am Gitta Goldberger," she answered joyfully, and directed us to her family's tent. She then ran to inform the other people of their group and they came out one by one, looking at us in amazement, as if we had come from the moon, and they touched us furtively to make sure that we were real. Then, unable to utter one single word and with tears running down their cheeks, they hugged us warmly.

"You are the first visitors we have had since we arrived here," Samuel Goldberger told us.

We had all forgotten the purpose of our coming and the parcels that we had brought. But our driver became impatient, and started to unload the truck. He entered the tent, looked around, saw everybody crying, and he too was so moved that he cried and shook hands with all the warm, affable people.

"Can you please help me to bring in the parcels?" he eventually asked. The tension was broken, and we were overwhelmed by all the volunteers, and by all the questions they asked us.

"How is the town of Alexandria? Is it a modern town? How many Jews live there? How many in Cairo? In the whole of Egypt? How are the people there? Are they nice? Did they also suffer during the war? Did they have enough food? Did the Egyptian Jews also have to run away during the war?

Do you, sister Thea, intend to return to Europe, or to go to Palestine?" This last question was one I hadn't decided on yet. But we tried to answer all their other questions to the best of our knowledge. I pitied those poor, destitute people who were so near to Cairo and Alexandria, and yet so far away, as if they were prisoners on the moon.

"And why, my God?" I asked myself. "Why are they in a detention camp? What have they done? Why can't these poor innocent people be free now that the war is over, after the long horrible nightmare they have lived through?" Again, the questions arrived in a phalanx and whizzed rapidly through my consciousness one after the other, and I had no answers.

We gave each of them his or her parcel, but they refused to open them then because they didn't want to miss one minute of being with us and talking to us. They told us about their sufferings and their expectations of being repatriated soon. They also hoped to meet members of their families, because they had been out of contact with them during the war, while they were away in Mauritius. We listened to them attentively and our hearts warmed up to them. However, after our long discourse, it was time to take leave, which we did with heavy hearts and with great regret. They begged us to stay a little longer, as we were the only link they had with the outside world, but we explained that we still had to drive to the ferry station where the man in charge had promised to wait for us, as we had to drive back to Port Taufiq in order to get the late train for Cairo. After having delivered all the surplus of our supplies to the administration officers, all these friendly people accompanied us to the gate, even the paralyzed man, with the help of two others. Again, and again we got many thanks, good-byes, and hugs. They promised to write to us after their return to their homes in Europe, and we promised to answer. We drove for a few hundred meters halted, and looked back with tears in our eyes, and saw the people still standing behind the barrier and waving their hands at us.

"Please come to see us again," Gitta Goldberger cried out to me at the gate, her beautiful fair hair seemed to wave at us too, "and please write to us." I waved back smiling and misty-eyed, knowing the wind would drive the first half of my promise away, as we would not be allowed by the authorities to visit them again.

We arrived at the ferry station where the boatman was waiting for us to re-cross the canal. We drove to the Port Taufiq railway station, and thanked Ali, the brave truck driver, for his goodwill tour. He kept muttering all the way back, "I don't understand it, they're not Bedouins or criminals, and yet they're locked up in the desert! Why? This can only be the *Afrit's* doing," he concluded.

"Yes, it was the doing of a kind of devil, by the name of Hitler," I explained to him. He shook his head in utter disgust and spat in the sand.

"*Allah Yikhalikom*! --May God preserve you, Dr. Lessing and Sister Thea," he said warmly, and stood by our side until we boarded the train to Cairo. "May God help you, for having helped those poor destitute people imprisoned in the middle of the desert." His looks showed he had not stopped wondering at the extraordinary phenomenon, as he waved a goodbye to us from the platform.

I arrived just before the night of Yom Kippur at my friends', the Sanders. There were many soldiers from the Jewish Brigade who were invited that evening, and we all took our last meal together before the great fast of the Judgment Day. The soldiers were impressed by the luxurious home and excellent traditional meal, served in beautiful porcelain and china, and excellent wine served in exquisite crystal glasses. They also admired the expensive original paintings on the walls and the good taste in the choice of sculptures and furniture.

I was exhausted, but couldn't help telling them about the poor Jews lost and lonely in the Sinai Desert. They were all fascinated by what they heard and asked many questions about their unfortunate brothers and sisters from Mauritius. After the dinner, I went to lie down, but I couldn't sleep. I went over what had happened in the last eventful thirty-six hours, hoping that the innocent prisoners in the clutches of the Sinai Desert would soon be freed. The next morning, I wrote urgent letters to the authorities in charge of the El-Shatt Camp, and implored them to release their inmates.

The sixty-four people were indeed repatriated after our visit to El-Shatt, but since, we never received news from any of them. I wonder why? We only heard later that they had had many difficulties and terrible shocks after their long-awaited return to their homes. Most of them didn't find any of their relatives alive. I suppose this must have been the cause of their silence.

Where are they all now, I wonder? What has become of golden-haired Gitta Goldberger and her family? These pages have already brought back some precious ghosts from the past; perhaps they will also bring back some of those wonderful people I met in the heart of the Sinai Desert.

29

LAST WISH

December 29, 1946 was a busy day, like every other day. There were urgent messages and calls coming in at all hours, and the consultation room, as usual, rapidly filled with patients, many of them seriously ill. I listened attentively to what each patient had to say, took down their names and particulars, and directed them to the doctor's room. At about twelve o'clock, when we had just finished our daily schedule in the minor Surgery Room, I was asked to answer an overseas call from London. I accepted the call, but the caller was unknown to me.

"Sister Thea," he cried frantically, "you must help me!"

I told him that there must be some mistake concerning his call, as I couldn't remember his name. He said I didn't know him, but that there was no mistake, and he insisted on talking to me, repeating my name urgently.

He told me the following: "I shall arrive together with

my ailing mother, Frieda Deutsch, on a British airliner at midnight on December 31st. Please help us," he pleaded, "I was told you are the only one who can help us."

"Just for the New Year," I thought. "There goes my holiday."

"I would like you to meet us at the airport in Heliopolis, and to please have an ambulance ready for transporting my mother to a hotel. Please reserve rooms for both my mother and me. Will you please fulfill my request?" he asked anxiously. "My mother has had a severe heart attack, and this is a matter of life and death." He urgently repeated his request twice in an entreating voice, and after some hesitation, I promised to make the necessary arrangements.

The whole affair seemed strange to me, as well as to everybody else with whom I discussed it. But I traveled to Cairo anyway, as I had promised, ordered a double room at the Shepherd's Hotel, and around eleven o'clock in the evening of December 31st an ambulance came to fetch me at my friend's home, and we drove to Heliopolis Airport. I was in my nurse's uniform so that the mother and son could recognize me.

The plane eventually landed, and Mrs. Deutsch was brought down on a stretcher. Her son, a tall, handsome young man, stood anxiously at her side and held her hand all the while. He breathed in relief when he saw me. We greeted each other and entered the ambulance. I saw an old, crippled woman before me, with delicate face and hands, who talked to me in German.

"I know that I'll soon die," she said weakly, "but before I

222 | ADA AHARONI

die, my last wish is to see my married daughter, who lives in Haifa, and whom I haven't seen since the Hitler period." She clutched my hand and looked at me entreatingly.

"Could you please help me to get to my daughter, Sister Thea?" she implored me. In confusion I nodded my head, while I thought, how in the world can I do that?

When we reached the passports control, it appeared that neither the mother nor the son had an entry visa to Egypt nor an entry visa to Palestine in their *laissez-passer*. They came from Holland, where they had lived a hair-raising underground existence all during the Nazi occupation. The mother had a single flight ticket: London-Cairo one way; the son had a ticket London-Cairo-London. Nothing else. The passport officer became angry and red in the face.

"How can one travel from one country to another without any visa? Is this a mockery?" He shouted at me. He was sure that this was my mother, accompanied by my brother, and he reprimanded me strongly for our irresponsible action.

"I definitely cannot let them leave the airport," he said bluntly.

I started to explain to him calmly, that first of all these two people were not my relatives; that I got a phone call at the Jewish Hospital in Alexandria two days before informing me about their arrival and about the purpose of their trip. "They are complete strangers, and I have never met them before. But I have promised to help them and so I will, and entreat you to help them too."

"But why are you doing this?" he asked in amazement. "Do they pay you for it?"

I explained that I was willing to fulfill their wish because I was a nurse and had to fulfill my duty as a nurse, "and as much as possible, every human being has to help if somebody is in distress," I added. "No, I do not get paid in money, but I get my payment in something much more precious than money--the wonderful feeling of having helped a human being."

He understood that my last phrase was directed to him, and looked at me sharply. "I assure you that the poor, sick woman will travel to Palestine as soon as possible," I pleaded, and the young man will fly back to London immediately after his mother's departure.

My pleading was not in vain. The brave officer's heart was filled with pity for these people, and then without further consultation or discussion with anybody else, he gave his okay for us and the ambulance to leave the airport. I couldn't believe my ears, and we hurried on our way before he would change his mind or be stopped by his superiors. But before leaving I asked him, if by chance, he would be on duty the next afternoon, so that there would be no difficulty for the sick lady to be transported onto the Misr Airline plane, bound for the Lydda Airport.

"I will be here," he assured me kindly, " and will myself take care of the whole operation, because by Allah, a thing like this doesn't happen every day, and I don't want to miss it!"

It was three o'clock in the morning when we arrived at the hotel. Mrs. Deutsch asked for a bath and a cup of tea, and then fortunately fell asleep. I drove home to my friends; they were still up, and eager to hear about my adventure. They were amazed by what they heard, and worried about how it would all end.

I was at the Shepherd's Hotel early in the morning to find out if the Misr Airline office was open, as we needed a plane ticket to Palestine for Mrs. Deutsch. It was closed. I found out the home address of the manager, called him over the phone, told him who I was and why I needed an urgent ticket to Lydda for that day's afternoon flight. He kindly agreed to come to the office, which was situated on the hotel's premises, though it was New Year's Day and he was on leave. On the way, down from his room to the office, Jacob, Mrs. Deutsch's son, told me that he also wanted a ticket to Lydda and back to Cairo with the same plane, so that he could accompany his mother. At that time, there was a shuttle service, Cairo-Lydda-Cairo; most of the passengers were officers of the British mandatory government. We got the tickets, thanked the benevolent manager for his kindness, and promised to inform him about the safe landing of the old lady, whose only wish was to see her daughter before leaving this earth.

I ordered an ambulance again. The same driver and stretcher bearer of the red cross 'secours d'urgence' were at the hotel about two o'clock. We greeted each other as if we were long-lost friends, and drove to the airport. And there he was, our passport officer, beaming jovially, ready to let the sick lady pass through and help her up the plane. But he also had to extend his kindness to the son, who wanted to accompany his mother to Lydda to be sure of her safe arrival, especially because she had no entry visa to Palestine. Jacob too, wished to see his sister Eva even from afar. She would probably be waiting for her mother at the airport, as we had sent her a cable informing her about her arrival. Jacob promised the officer he would return to Cairo with the same plane. The magnanimous officer closed his eyes in bewilderment for a moment and puckered his thick brows disapprovingly.

"Okay," he said at length, "but under one condition, that Sister Thea stays at the airport to keep me company until the young man returns from the trip."

I agreed, and he pulled out a chair for me, and made me some delicious hot tea, with fresh mint leaves from his own garden. I bought the *Egyptian Gazette* newspaper and the *Bourse Egyptienne* and he wanted me to tell him all the news I read in them, while we patiently waited for the return of the Misr Airline plane from Lydda. Now and then I chatted with Mabrouk, the passport officer, who told me about his wife Fawzia and his nine children living in Choubra. "All my boys want to be passport officers," he said, smiling a warm, fatherly smile.

"What about the girls?" I asked.

"Even the girls," he said ruefully. "But I told both the boys and girls they'd better choose safer and more lucrative professions. The things that can happen here, you wouldn't believe it! And what they pay you is peanuts in comparison with the headaches this job gives you! You wouldn't believe it!" he repeated.

"I would," I said, nodding my head.

His smile became broader and we went on chatting together. The hours passed, the plane arrived, and Jacob stepped out. Both Mabrouk and I heaved a sigh of relief. He passed through the pass control, took both the officer's hands and then mine, and kissed them warmly, tears running unashamedly down his cheeks. I was moved by the sight, and felt my own would soon gush forth if I didn't check them hard.

We drove into town, where we had a cup of that special coffee at Groppi's, which was the best place in the whole of Cairo for delicious beverages and ice cream. It was a favorite place too for the Allied Forces, who never missed a chance for an excellent meal at Groppi's. Their coffee had a delicious aroma and was exactly what I needed after such a trying experience. It was already late, and Jacob wanted to go to a synagogue for evening prayers; his plane was due to depart after midnight. I accompanied him to the main grand synagogue, the impressive *Shaar Hashamayim* in Adli street, where he prayed and thanked God for having helped his mother, with the aid of the charitable Mabrouk, to reach her daughter in Palestine. When we came out, he hugged me and thanked me warmly for all I did for them.

"Without you, dear Sister Thea," he said kindly, "mother would have died without having seen Eva, and I would never have forgiven myself. You have given her joy, and to me you have rendered a especially great service--my peace of mind for the years to come. God bless you!"

We said good-bye to each other, and he promised to keep in touch. And indeed, for many years I received a Hanukkah greeting from him. I returned to my friends and they heaved sighs of relief when they heard the happy end of the story.

I informed the hospital that all went well, and that I would be coming back the next day. I also called the Manager of the Misr Airline office, reported all that had happened, and gave him many thanks from me and the Deutsches. We had all done a good team's work together to benefit an old, sick woman. Again, the call of humanity had surpassed barriers of creeds, beliefs, and even laws. The beautiful cooperation between Egyptian Moslems and Jews has been fully successful.

I visited Frieda Deutsch in Haifa on the Hadar Hacarmel, in Massada Street, after my arrival there in February 1947. She felt much better after her arrival in Haifa, and she lived happily with her daughter Eva, surrounded by six vivacious grandchildren. A broad smile of joy and gratefulness beamed all over her face when she saw me. She passed away some months later, but her bright smile remains in me.

30

LUXOR AND THE MENA HOUSE

During my holiday in 1946, I made a trip to Upper Egypt. I was astounded by the beauty of the temples at Karnak, Luxor, Idfu, Kom-Ombo, and especially by the majestic palace of Queen Hatshepsut, in the middle of the desert. I was greatly impressed by this formidable queen who had successfully made peace with her neighbors, and had sent peace messengers to all the territories in her vast empire to give the people their lands back and to sign peace treaties with her. On one of her huge, impressive obelisks, built five thousand years ago made of granite from Aswan, she engraved, "It is the wiser and stronger sovereign who makes peace, than he who makes war."

Sound and wise words, astonishingly so, in a period when war was thought of as a sign of greatness. Her philosophy was an inspiration for the peace treaty effected between

Egypt and Israel in 1978. President Sadat visited Queen Hatshepsut's palace before he went to sign the Camp David Accord with President Carter and Prime Minister Begin, and he said that her spirit of peace greatly inspired him. I hope this peace-loving queen's message will spread in all our war-ravaged modern world.

I also admired the beautiful, gigantic torso of Rameses II at Memphis; he was the pharaoh thought to be the one who reigned at the time of Moses. The exquisite sculptures of daily life, birds, animals, and nature scenes by first-class sculptors at Sakkara were astonishing, as well as the impressive head of Akhenaten, the royal dreamer and son of the Sun, on the banks of the Nile at Luxor. I was also impressed by Osiris, the judge of man's soul, at the temple of Idfu, with the falcon-headed Horus standing on guard at the enormous gate. The sculpture of Isis and Nephtys, her sister, with the faithful Anubis, the dog or jackal, watcher of the graves, crouching at their feet greatly impressed me. The colossal columns adorned with scarabs and lotus flowers at Karnak, Thebes, and other temples were also marvelous. One of the grandiose things which especially caught my attention was Queen Cleopatra's huge pink, unfinished obelisk, which was abandoned when it was only one-third excavated. I thoughtfully walked over it, thinking of brave Cleopatra's decision to cuddle a poisonous snake in her bosom, rather than be Caesar's captive.

I was so entranced by the pharaonic sculpture and excellent art, that I decided on my return from Upper Egypt to visit again the museum of Tutankhamen in Cairo. I wandered wide-eyed among the hieroglyphics, papyrus, and the golden treasures artistically inlaid with precious stones, lapis lazuli, and mother of pearl, and thought to myself: The pharaohs believed in the afterlife, and they have succeeded in attaining it! Here I am, wandering among them, and I now know how they lived, how they educated their children, how they worked, looked, and how they thought! I gazed into the uncanny, shining lifelike glass eyes of a life-sized sculptured pharaonic farmer couple, found in an amazing well-preserved condition, with original coloring, clothes, and all--and felt as if they were about to talk to me. For me five thousand years later, they are still alive, I thought, and their rich culture still enriches my mind and soul! And suddenly these thoughts were accompanied by feelings of confusion, inferiority, and guilt: What will *we* leave to our descendants five thousand years hence? Just the remains of atomic weapons and nuclear bombs, if humanity will still exist then? Where are our beautiful monuments, temples, palaces, and sculptures which will survive that long? The Eiffel tower suddenly came to mind; and I was ashamed of the comparison.

***

On that occasion, I visited my friends, the Lipsky family, in Cairo. They had lived there since their escape from Nazi Germany, on their way to Shanghai. They had, with our aid, simply stepped down from the ship during its stopover in Port Said, and had adjusted pretty well to life in Egypt. They were happy to see me and they informed me I had a phone call from Dr. Katz.

I contacted him immediately, and he told me to stay in Cairo to take over the nursing of a famous antique dealer who was a good friend of King Farouk's. He was suffering from a brain hemorrhage and was reported to have been unconscious for some time, but was now out of the coma. Mr. Sayed Bey was a good-natured and intelligent man in his mid-sixties, and I liked taking care of him. His wife was Italian, and she called herself "the white moon of Calabria," the place she came from. She tried to convince him to call her by that name, but never succeeded. They had two beautiful daughters, Cleopatra and Alexandra. They lived in a large, gorgeous, palatial building in the center of Cairo. The ground floor was an antique hall, that looked like a well-stocked storeroom of a museum. I loved going there, where I continued my education and dialogue with pharaonic culture. The first floor of the house was the living quarter of the family. I stayed with them for about three weeks, and they were all very kind to me.

At the end of this period, my patient finally was on his feet again, and his physicians advised him that he should be transferred to the Mena House at Giza for his convalescence. So, the whole family moved to the Mena House, where a luxurious suite was rented for them for three weeks. They invited me to go with them, and to go on caring for the Bey, and I accepted. All the rooms had balconies with a beautiful view of the Sphinx and the three Pyramids, standing like huge tents at the opening of the desert. My patient sat on the balcony for hours and stared thoughtfully at them. We often had long conversations, mainly about the war, and I confided in him that I still had hope of finding my parents and sister.

Sometimes I rolled him in his wheelchair through the luscious park and gardens of the Mena House, which we all thoroughly enjoyed. King Farouk paid him several visits at the time. Their lively conversation inevitably turned around scarabs, as King Farouk owned a precious collection of ancient scarabs--the pharaoh's symbol of life. The dung beetle which came out of the earth, was considered an example of what happened to the soul of man, when he was resurrect-ed from the earth into spirit. This is how the ordinary dung beetle became a holy scarab.

Even after World War Two, there were many American officers still stationed in Egypt; and some of them were living at the Mena House. They were strong, vigorous and handsome, and loved playing tennis. Another inmate also living there, was King Zogu from Albania, with his Hungar-ian-born wife, their little son, his older unmarried sisters, as well as several of his cabinet ministers. They always sat together around a large round table, and rarely talked among themselves, or to anyone else. I felt sorry for them, as they looked depressed, lost and lonely. Each of their looks and gestures bespoke the tragedy of their banishment. I was particularly sorry for Queen Zogu, who had a tender and fine complexion and sorrowful eyes.

It was very hot during the day, but in the evenings a cool, dry desert wind blew from the Pyramids. Then the social life of the Mena House was at its peak. Everybody in the wonderful park and the gardens of the hotel sat there chatting, sometimes until the early morning hours. This is when I had my most interesting conversations with Sayed Bey, and I learned a great deal about antiques and about his business as an antique dealer, as well as about life in Egypt in general. I was an avid listener and drank in every one of his wise words. The Bey and his wife were so pleased with my treatment that they presented me with a fine piece of ancient sculpture as a memento.

"This is exactly what we need for the Hospital's dining room," I said happily.

"But, Thea," the White Moon of Calabria cried, "this is for you, not for the dining room."

"My joy is doubled when I share it with others," I said. She did not seem convinced, but her husband nodded knowingly.

31

A BIBLICAL DINOSAUR

One day one of the polite, attentive waiters at the Mena House, in white garb and red sash, overheard me saying that I intended to make a trip to Palestine very soon. He came over to me and in surprisingly fluent English, told me an astonishing thing:

"I am from a nearby village by the name of Mena," he said, "where there lived at the time of the Bible a famous Pharaoh. In our village, situated on the shores of the Nile, is an old legend which has been told from father to son for generations, about Miriam, one of the Pharaoh's daughters. Miriam liked to walk along the shores of the Nile with her handmaids, and during one of her walks she saw a small straw crib floating on the Nile amid the papyrus, and heard the whining of a baby. She ordered her servants to pull the crib ashore, and inside it found to her surprise, a beautiful, strong baby boy crying. The baby was brought to her father's palace, where he was nursed and educated, and he was named Moussa, or Moses, which means *stranger*. Moses in time became the leader of the Jewish people living in bondage during the rule of Pharaoh Menaptah. Eventually he got permission from the Pharaoh to leave Egypt with the Jewish people for their Promised Land. Since then, all the first-born sons in Mena Village are called Moussa, and this why I too am named Moussa," he ended. "Do they know that in Palestine?" he asked.

"But this is extraordinary!" I cried in surprise, "No, Moussa, I don't think they know what you have just told me in Palestine, or anywhere else in the world!" I felt as if the Moussa before me were a living relic linking me back to pharaonic times and to the Bible.

When I related this story to Sayed Bey, he was amazed and said he had vaguely heard about it.

"But this is like discovering a Biblical dinosaur, that is still alive!" I cried in astonishment. "Sometimes you wonder if these legends in the Bible are true, and here you have a living proof that this one has indeed happened!"

Sayed Bey smiled and said, "A Biblical dinosaur, or a living scarab, it is still to be seen, but what amazes me most is that even Egyptian Moslems, follow this tradition, and still call their first-born sons *Moussa* to this day!"

I hope one day an academic delegation will travel to Mena Village to research this story. I am sure Moussa, the waiter of Mena House Hotel, would gladly help them, if he is still around.

When I left Egypt for Israel in February 1947, I sent a postcard of Jerusalem from Israel addressed to *Moussa, Mena*

House, working on the first floor. I hope he got it. In it I wrote:

To Dear Moussa,

This is where Moussa-Moses sent his people after wandering for forty years in the Sinai Desert. I hope you will be able to visit us one day. In the meantime, I send my best wishes to you and your family, and to all the Moussa-Moses of Mena Village, who are a living relic of the great, ancient, Biblical times.

Sincerely,
Sister Thea Wolf

32

AYOUB THE FAITHFUL

Ayoub served his master, Dr. Katz, faithfully for more than ten years. He was about thirty years old, had only one wife, two boys and a little daughter. His family lived in a village on the shores of the Mahmoudieh Canal, and he went to pay them a visit once a week on his day off.

He lived in a small room on the roof of the house, where his master had his apartment, on one of the main streets in Alexandria. Ayoub only talked when he was asked a question, or had a task to do and wanted to know how to go about it. He always walked in slippers in the apartment, in order to make as little noise as possible. He was polite, thoughtful, modest, a perfect handyman, and a truthful and devoted servant. In his eyes, his master came immediately in line after Allah.

One Sunday morning I got an urgent call from Ayoub, telling me that his master, the *Rais*, was very sick, that he was worried, and that I should come straight away. I went immediately, and I found that poor Dr. Katz was suffering from a severe lung infection. Antibiotics didn't exist at that time, and he had to be treated in the old-fashioned manner, which lasted a few weeks. I looked after him during all that period. Ayoub continued to do his regular duty as usual, but he looked very unhappy and was deeply worried.

One morning, Ayoub sank down on a chair in the kitchen, his head between his hands. He didn't eat breakfast, didn't do his daily work, and even refused to say good morning either to me or to his *Rais*. When I asked him for the reason of his strange behavior, he looked at me with large sad eyes, and didn't answer. In the past, he had never failed to come to work, he had never complained, he had always been *mabsut* (happy). He repeated his strange behavior for a few more days, and when I told him that the *Rais* was angry with him because he didn't inquire how he felt, he burst out and said in a hoarse voice, talking rapidly, now and then interrupted by a moan which made me shudder, "Oh, I know the truth now. I know that my master is going to die, I know it for sure. And therefore, it's my duty to receive him, when he comes up to heaven. I have to be there before him. I have to prepare everything for him!"

I was taken aback by this outburst. It was the last thing I would have expected. All my assurances, as well as everybody else's who visited the sick *Rais*--the physicians, the nurses, and all his friends--that in a few days his master would be well and out of bed, were in vain. Ayoub shook his head and sadly said again, "I know better than you, than all of you. My master will surely die; I saw it in a dream, where Allah appeared to me in all his glory and ordered me to come quickly so that I could prepare the way for my beloved *Rais,* and Allah cannot be fooled."

"But your *Rais* feels better!" I cried in desperation. "Come and see for yourself." But he wouldn't listen.

"He will die," he repeated with finality, and went up silently to his room.

We tried to coax him into drinking and eating something, but it was of no avail. The poor, demented man became thinner and thinner, paler and paler every day. He didn't do any work at all, and just sat limply like a loose bundle on a chair in the kitchen and stared at the wall all day long.

"Come to the hospital, and we'll look after you," I tried to coax him. But I knew already before opening my mouth that all my efforts would fall on deaf ears.

Ayoub just looked through me, as if I didn't exist.

One morning he didn't show up, and I got alarmed. I went up to his room and knocked, but there was no answer. I tried to force the door, but it didn't budge. At length, I called the police. We all went up to his room, opened the door, and there we found him; he had strangled himself. He was on his way to heaven.

His *Rais* recovered a few days later, and only then did we tell him the story about Ayoub and his fateful decision. He was deeply shocked and saddened by the tragedy which had befallen his faithful servant.

"But couldn't you have forced him to eat?" he cried in exasperation.

"Believe me, we did everything we could," I said quietly.

"Mohammed even came on purpose from the hospital yesterday to try to feed him by force, or to bring him to the hospital so that we could treat him there, but Ayoub refused everything categorically, and vomited on purpose anything we forced into his mouth. But that he would hang himself-- this nobody had predicted."

Dr. Katz looked at me with pain in his eyes. "I'll never have another Ayoub," he murmured. "He was not only a faithful servant, but also a faithful friend. I will miss him so."

Ayoub left a remembrance behind him. For years he was in charge of three bottles of champagne, the only ones left over all throughout World War Two. We kept them to celebrate Victory Day. Victory Day 1945 came at last, and the three bottles of champagne were joyfully put on ice to cool. Dr. Katz opened them, and we were all surprised that no white foam came out, and the cork didn't burst. We sipped the "champagne," and to our great surprise it was pure water! Ayoub had celebrated his own Victory Day and refilled the bottles with Nile water! Maybe he thought this was the right drink for his historic trip from this world to the next. And maybe the question about what happened to the three bottles of champagne, was the first one his master asked him, when they met in heaven twenty-four years later.

33

GOOD-BYE ALEXANDRIA

After World War Two was over all the foreign armies: the American, British, Australian, South African, the Jewish Brigade, the Czechoslovakian, the exiled Poles, the Free French, and the Italian and Greek people, all began to leave the hospitable Land of the Nile, many of them with deep regret. They had all grown to like the warm Egyptian people and their sunny, hospitable country.

We, Jewish refugees, who were fortunate to have found an adopted homeland in Egypt, were terribly anxious to get a sign from our families in Europe. Despite all our efforts, we had been unable to save them from deportation; but we hoped, nevertheless, that they may have miraculously survived. But slowly the bad news arrived for nearly all the European staff members, from various organizations where we had inquired about the whereabouts of our families. Whole families had been deported to Auschwitz, Maidanek,

Theresienstadt, Sobibor, Bergen-Belsen and various other concentration camps, and since then, nothing else was heard about them. Sometimes the definite facts took years to arrive.

Only in 1947, did I finally get the same tragic news concerning my father, my mother, my sister and her four-year-old son, my uncles, aunts, cousins; all together seventy-two family members who perished in the infamous Nazi gas showers and ovens. Only three people remained alive: A cousin of my father's and his daughter--he returning from Theresienstadt, she from Birkenau-- met accidentally in the corridor of a hospital in Koln. Another cousin of my father's survived in Theresienstadt Ghetto. That was all that remained of a large and well-established family that had lived in Germany as good and diligent citizens for more than three hundred years.

The atrocious pain, guilt, helplessness, and feeling of utter loss were unbearable. The tragedy of my family who had perished in the Holocaust clutched at my throat, its grip gradually closing on it, throughout the additional year that I remained in Egypt. I became very depressed and felt totally alienated and alone. I could not forgive my former German fellow creatures for their cruelty, for burning six million of my brothers and sisters and killing so many others.

I lifted my head to the skies and saw myriads of martyred people, wounded, mutilated, their features scorched by fire and distorted by gas, their naked emaciated bodies pointing accusing fingers, their pleading eyes fixed on me. I raised my bewildered eyes to the stars and asked: "Why? Oh, my God? What was the use of all this horrible slaughter of innocents?"

But the stars are far away, they do not hear us; and even if they did, they would just go on glittering. What does poured blood of six million people mean to a star? Not a drop of blood reaches it or splatters onto its brilliance. It remains clean, twinkling and totally unconcerned. I was confirmed in my belief that the sooner we decided that our fate lies in our hands and not in the stars or what lies behind them--so much the better for us.I felt I had to make a decisive choice soon, to go where I could stay for good--in my own land, where no one would tell me, "Thea, you don't belong here, you're a stranger, a freak, a spy. We can gas you and burn you, as well as all your family, and *no one*, none of all the nations in the world will lift a finger to help you, just because you happen to be Jewish."

There came days when the sad melody from Om Kulthum's rich throat *"ya leili, ya leili,"* "my night, my night" coming through my window, painful and deep, seemed the natural accompaniment to the sounds of my broken soul. At night the grave faces of my father, mother, sister, uncles, aunts, and cousins continued to haunt me, floating interminably through my brain. Sometimes they waved at me and looked piercingly, a smoldering question on their burning lips, "Thea, why didn't you save us?" I felt my world was disintegrating, and that I was losing my place in the universe.

I was alive, and they weren't! My God, how could I live with this knowledge? How had it happened? The deep guilt of having remained alive while they were dead gnawed at my bones and heart. At length, I decided I owed it to them to go to Israel, the land of our forefathers, our real land, where

Jews would not be molested again. I owed it not only to my family and relatives, but also to all the millions who were not alive anymore, and who had suffered Jewish martyrs' deaths. I owed it too to the future generations.

I said good-bye to the beautiful palm trees and pink and red roses in our garden, to the pale Egyptian moon, the blue skies and the bright shining sun, and informed my superiors at the Hospital about my decision. The whole hospital staff were upset, but they understood, and when they saw I had made up my mind, they stopped trying to convince me to stay. They all told me that in case I couldn't find my place in Israel, I should immediately return to Egypt and would always be welcome there.

"Dear Thea, the doors are open before you, whenever you would like to come back," Dr. Katz said warmly, and I detected an unusual disturbed and sad note in his seemingly calm voice. Some of the nurses said that I probably would come back 'home' soon, after having overcome my depression. But I shook my head sorrowfully, knowing I would not return. I was moved to see how much the staff was attached to me, but I stuck to my decision.

"The hospital will not be the same without you," Princess Toussoun said, at the farewell party they gave in my honor.

Before I left Alexandria, she brought me a lovely present which I preciously cherish to this very day. She graciously smiled at and presented me with a beautifully hand-sewn napkin decorated with an elaborate ancient Egyptian design. It was skillfully adorned with silver and colored silk threads, which she herself had personally stitched for me. I was deeply touched by her gesture and hugged her closely. She represented a precious part of the "Inter-Cultural Hospital Symphony" which had greatly enriched me, and which I unfortunately had to leave behind, geographically, but not spiritually. She, and the brave Egyptian women and men who helped me to save thousands of Jews from the atrocious Nazi Holocaust, as related in some of the precious stories--will always be in my heart and my memories.

I started to prepare for my departure. Everything went smoothly, except getting a visitor's visa from the British authorities in Cairo. At this time the British "White Book," which limited Jewish immigration into Palestine, was still in force, and it was impossible to obtain a visa. I decided to leave without it. I said good-bye to all my dear friends and colleagues, who had become as part of my family, and I left Alexandria by train. I first voyaged to Cairo, and from there took the night train to Haifa.

I knew the sleeping car man in charge; he had once been treated at our hospital, and was the same man who had helped me in getting Karl into Sudan, and several illegal fugitives into Palestine. I gave him my passport and told him that I was tired and a bit ailing, and that I would leave all my suitcases outside the cabin for the custom's control at the Kantara Station, because I wanted to try to get some sleep. I was nervous and in a sad mood. Leaving behind fifteen years of a very fruitful period of my life and many, many good friends, was a much harder task than I had thought.

I fell asleep for a while. The train came to a halt, and suddenly, there was a loud knock at the door of my sleeping compartment. A strong voice called out, "Sister Thea, Sister Thea, open the door please, this is Abdel Rahman, the customs' officer. I was told that you don't feel well. And if so, I wish to travel with you to Jerusalem and to bring you there to the hospital, I don't want you to travel alone."

I opened the door, and there was Abdel Rahman, who some time before had also been hospitalized at our hospital. He was so upset by the news that I was sick that he forgot to do his duty and to ask me for my visa. I was moved by his offer of help, and felt guilty that I pretended to be sick, especially after his faith in me. But there was no other way out. I assured him that I felt much better already, that I was able to travel on my own, and that friends were waiting for me in Haifa and were going to take good care of me. I thanked him warmly for his good intentions, and bade him farewell and Godspeed.

"God bless you, Schwester Thea," he said, smiling the charming, typical warm and kind-hearted Egyptian smile I shall never forget.

It was already morning. The sun came out, but it did not change my mood. I still felt sad and gloomy but determined. I arrived in Haifa, where my kind friends were waiting for me at the railway station and welcomed me warmly. I looked at the blue skies and already started to feel at home. In April 1947, I began working as a surgery nurse at the Government Schweitzer Hospital in Tiberias. I tried to adapt myself to the new surroundings, new challenges, other working conditions, and also the renewing of old friendships after many years of separation. I was satisfied to be able to contribute a bit to aiding my people in Palestine, but still depressed by the terrible tragedy that had befallen my family.

Every Friday evening, I went down to the main post office in Tiberias to place a call to Alexandria, either to friends or to the hospital. The telephone operators in Tiberias, and also in Alexandria, always did their best to get me through to the wanted phone number. We talked for a few minutes; we were happy to hear each other's voices, but we all knew that something was going to explode soon, when the British Mandate would end in May 1948, and the State of Israel would be established, according to United Nations' decision. Before that, in November 1947, a bi-national State for Israelis and Palestinians has been suggested, but the Palestinians refused. This meant that when the British would retire from Palestine, there would be a war between Jews and Arabs.

One of those hot summer mornings I got a call from the Egyptian embassy in Jerusalem. The speaker on the phone urged me, "Sister Thea, go back quickly to Egypt, because you would be safer there than in Israel. Believe me, many friends of yours are very worried about you in Alexandria." He even proposed to send me an embassy car which would come to Tiberias specially for me, and drive me to the Haifa railway station. I felt very touched and thank him for his good intention. It recalled the close ties I left behind me in Egypt, and the gentle, warm people who cared for me there. But all the same, I decided that my place now was in Israel. I told him kindly that I was unable to travel at that time, and begged him to thank my friends for their warm concern for my safety.

I also received a letter from my good Greek friends, the Kyriakopouloses from Mansoura, urging me to return immediately to Egypt because a war was inevitable, and that I would be safer with them in Mansoura. These prophecies were not fulfilled, until May 1948. The great modern Exodus of Jews began in Egypt, and unfortunately even my gentile friends the Kyriakopouloses of Mansoura had to leave. All of them had been born and brought up in Mansoura, and I was sorry to hear that they too, had to go through the extremely painful ordeal of upheaval and uprootedness. I was glad that I had remained in Israel, where I felt my roots penetrating the beloved soil deeper from day to day.

34

JULIUS JOSEF IN TIBERIAS

I had another important reason for not wanting to leave Tiberias at that time. I met Dr. Julius Levinsohn, a kind and gentle German-Jewish lawyer, who had also lost his only sister in the Holocaust. We became close friends and he eventually asked me to marry him. Until then, my career had been my main occupation and love, and whenever I was wooed by a suitor and asked in marriage, I just laughed and pushed my suitors out of my way. But now it was different. After having lost all my family, I felt I needed somebody close of my very own to rely upon, and Julius too needed me. We became closer and closer and eventually, decided to get married. It was a bright spot in an otherwise dark period of my life.

With my loving and thoughtful husband at my side, the dark, bitter cloud which had enveloped me like a shroud during my last year in Alexandria gradually drifted away. The birds twittered in the trees and the sun shone in the skies again. Humanity seemed once more vital and radiant. My fear of the jungle in the heart of man was gone. I identified with people again; they were my brothers and sisters once more; I pitied the sick and the wounded, and wanted to help them.

"After all it was the Allies not the Nazis who won," Julius reflected. "The devil himself can do nothing to a human being, as long as he has faith in man and life." How wise Julius was and what a source of strength!

I became a fighter again, on the side of life. I heard the call of humankind, imperious, irresistible, like a command, "Thea, where are you?" it cried. I sprang to my feet, "*Hineni*! Here I am!" I answered the call, reinforced by my kind, intelligent and supporting companion at my side. He helped me to dispel rancor, transform indecision, and renew the spirit. He strengthened me in my difficult endeavor of consciously separating the past from the future.

I rejoiced again every time patients recovered, and gradually gained my assurance and self-esteem. Together with Julius, we decided to take care of my Uncle Jacob and his daughter Meta, who had settled again in Köln and who were in urgent need of money and clothes, and of letters from me telling them about life in Israel. He returned from Theresienstadt, and Meta returned from Auschwitz-Birkenau. They met after the liberation in a hospital in Köln, Germany. I wrote to them about my marriage, about my wonderful Julius, my work as head nurse in the operating rooms of the hospital in Tiberias, and as an instructor to the student nurses. I promised Uncle Jacob and Meta that as soon as possible I would come to pay them a visit. It took a few years until I could fulfil my promise, but all that time I had the good feeling again that I was not alone. I had found a faithful and loving mate, and now, a family. We decided to look after uncle and cousin as if they were my father and sister, and we remained very close to them until the angel of death took them away.

I eventually learned what happened to my parents. Years later, I saw my father's picture in a Lodz concentration camp under rather strange circumstances. In 1954, I was in Essen, Germany, with my late husband, who had a law office for restitution claims for Jews who were in Nazi concentration camps. One day, one of our clients, Mr. Kohn, showed me a picture, and he asked me if I could help him in finding the relatives of one of the men in the picture. He pointed to a man wearing a special hat.

"Where was the picture taken, and what is the name of this man?" I asked him, in utter amazement.

"It was taken in the ghetto of Lodz. I was deported there from Berlin, but I was born in Essen. This man was also from Essen; his name was Moritz Wolf."

"That is my father's name!" I cried, aghast. Mr. Kohn looked at me with disbelief. Our secretaries in the office knew about the fate of my parents, and they stopped working on hearing the painful conversation. Our archives' clerk took out his handkerchief, brought it to his eyes, and quickly left the room. I couldn't breathe for a few moments and felt as if I were choking.

"Did the man in the picture have a wife?" I asked at length

breathlessly.

"Yes," he said sadly, "her name was Jenny. She always talked about her daughter Thea, who was a nurse in Egypt, and she always believed that Thea would one day save them."

"I am Thea, their daughter!" I cried out, clutching my throat in pain, while brimming tears flowed down my cheeks. Mr. Kohn watched me with pity in his eyes, when it dawned on him that I was indeed Thea Wolf, daughter of Moritz and Jenny Wolf.

I looked at the picture of my father, and kissed it spontaneously, holding back my tears in fear that they would soil the picture. "What kind of work did the people in the picture do?" I asked at length.

"They were probably building roads," he said slowly.

"But what happened to them?" I asked, aghast.

Mr. Kohn couldn't tell me anything more, because he was later deported to Auschwitz, where he was put in charge of the telegraph stations, and thus he remained alive. I never found out how my father and mother died, but it was not difficult to guess.

When Mr. Kohn left, my husband, who had heard all the painful conversation, took me in his arms and hugged me like a baby. At that moment my tears gushed out again, "Why, my Lord, why? They were such gentle and good people!"

"At least we still have each other," Julius said softly, and he kissed me gently on my forehead and hair, wiping my tears with his handkerchief. I made a great effort to check my tears, and I kissed him back, "at least we still have each other," I sobbed, but was deeply shaken.

All the hurt at the injustice of what had befallen my family and the Jewish people, came back to me, my bones melted again, my teeth rocked in my gums loosely, the phalanx in my mind, started rushing again, all armed with pointed lance-questions: "Where were you, Thea? Why didn't you save them?" Burning accusations burnt my nights and scorched my lips and eyes: "You are alive! They are not!"

My dear Julius did everything in his power to bring me back to myself. Pointing to the silvery waters of the Jordan River, he said gently, "The flow of the river is only in one direction Thea, like our lives.... It is not in our power to turn the flow back, we are only humans.... But it is in our power to make our lives significant, beautiful and meaningful...." He also pointed to the red, blue, white and violet anemones popping their merry heads in the grass and whispered lovingly, "Every one of them, vibrating with life, can be a source of joy for us, or merely a fading flower--it all depends on us...."

Kissing my cheek gently in the breeze, kind, loving Julius, eventually instilled in me a deep love of the beauties of nature around the Sea of Galilee, and it started chanting warm melodies of life in my heart. The Jordan with its soothing turquoise-blue hues, splashed in my veins, and bathed my soul like a soothing balm. The song of life overcame that of death, and I retrieved my place among those who believe in a world beyond war and courageously struggle to bring it about.

35

MICHAEL

Shortly after my arrival in Tiberias in April 1947, I was blessed with a jewel, a young boy of twelve by the name of Michael. His original name was Gerd Wolf, and his grandmother Rosa was a second cousin of my father's. I found Michael in a kibbutz, just by chance. We had the same name, and a good friend of mine who was in that Kibbutz pointed him out to me, and asked me if we were related. I sat on a bench on a dark night with Michael at my side for the first time. I looked in his direction, and he in mine. He suddenly hugged me in the dark and said, "You look like my mother." How could he have seen in the dark? I couldn't resist my tears, and there and then, I decided to adopt him.

Michael's mother and father had been killed during a raid of the German Wehrmacht in a Yugoslavian forest. The Nazis tried to kill him too, but because he was small the bullet passed over his head, and he was saved. He fell beneath the

Find thousands of unique
items in our online shop
www.oxfam.org.uk/shop

OXFAM

VAT: 348 4542 38

**Volunteer here: Have fun,
meet new people & learn
new skills**
Sign up in-store or at
www.oxfam.org.uk/jointheteam

MILLIE	SALES	F4674/POS1
FRIDAY 8 DECEMBER 2023		11:53 132524
1 OTHER BOOKS		£1.49

1 Items

TOTAL	**£1.49**
CASH	£1.50
CHANGE	£0.01

Oxfam Shop: F4674
14, High Street,
Tenterden, TN30 6AP
01580 765326
oxfam.org.uk/shop

corpses and when he heard the soldiers say, "Let's go, our job is done, they're all dead," he scrambled out and hid in the forest. He at length arrived at the home of some benevolent Yugoslavian farmers, and they fed and raised him as their own son. Michael was thus saved; he was only ten then.

We immediately felt attached to each other, Michael and I, and he became my son. Michael today is happily married and has three wonderful children. When my dear husband died, and it was a great loss to me, thanks to Michael, I am not alone. I am grateful for all the happiness I receive from Michael and his family and from all my good friends. Together with my voluntary work at the "Open House" in Jerusalem, Michael and his family, his lively Yemenite wife and his 'tsabra' Israeli-born children--all fill my life with meaning and joy.

36

DR. KATZ

After King Farouk was forced to abdicate in 1952, the Hospital of the Jewish Community in Alexandria continued to function for a few years under the new regime. Several doctors and nurses left, and local personnel took over, but unfortunately Gamal-Abd-El-Nasser decided to give it its death blow in 1960.

An additional terrible thing happened just before the closure of the Hospital. The chief surgeon, our dear, excellent Dr. Katz, was arrested in Cairo when returning from a visit to Switzerland in midsummer 1959, on false pretenses that he was a spy for Israel--he who had been so far from politics all his life, and so uninvolved in anything which did not concern his medical profession! This time the witch-hunt was relentless. The state prosecutor condemned him to the death penalty, and later, the punishment was changed to lifelong penal servitude. It was a terrible period for him and for all his friends, and his health greatly suffered.

He was at length liberated after eighteen long months in prison, through continuous intervention from the German federal government and written declarations from many friends who proclaimed him innocent of all the accusations against him. I, too, did my best to personally intervene on his behalf through the German Foreign Office in Bonn. I went on purpose to Bonn to see them and wrote to them continuously that they had to do everything in their power to free Dr. Katz. He was at last freed, but from then on he was a weak, broken, and uprooted man. He passed away in March 1969, in Athens, after having contracted a severe lung condition during his imprisonment. He who had saved so many lives during his lifetime couldn't be saved by anyone. All over the world his many friends wept bitter tears when they heard about his sad end. I tried to see him before he died but I arrived too late.

When President Nasser ordered the nationalization of the Jewish Hospital in Alexandria, as well as the one in Cairo, all the staff had to leave. It was the end of a gloriously humane enterprise.

***

Today, the building of the Jewish Hospital in Alexandria is used as a students' dormitory. Probably, the students there have never heard about the marvelous work accomplished at the inter-cultural Hospital of the Jewish Community in Alexandria, about Dr Katz, or about any of the excellent staff who all worked harmoniously and so fruitfully together to save people's lives.

* * *

Perhaps these lines will leave a frail trail of rose petals in the memory of Excellent Doctor Katz and all his wonderful staff., and for all those future doctors who can benefit from his example. He was a role model for all the medical profession.

War and conflict have no pity, I thought sorrowfully, they cruelly cut down the best of us when we still can give so much. Goodbye my brother, may your memory fare well, dear, excellent Dr Katz.

37

INDEPENDENCE

Israel's War of Independence began when its half a million inhabitants were attacked by its Arab neighbors. For some time Tiberias was completely cut off. There were house-to-house attacks in the lower part of Tiberias, and wounded civilians were brought to the hospital all through the day and night. The hospital was the only one for the town of Tiberias, the Jordan Valley, and the Galilee settlements, and for some time also for the town of Safad. We worked nonstop day and night with fear in our hearts, but finally we could celebrate Israel's first Independence Day, on May 15, 1948.

Looking back on my life today, like a strip of film stretched backwards before my eyes, or the gushing waters of the Nile--I realize that war has always dogged me and haunted me throughout my years. During the First World War, I was a starved child wandering with cramps in my stomach, desperately seeking for forgotten raw potatoes in the fields. As a nurse in Alexandria, I lived through the horrors of World War II, and suffered the unspeakable tragedy of having my whole family murdered by the Nazis. Since I have been in Israel, my life has been torn by war after war--five cruel and senseless wars in which young blood, on both sides of the frontier, was pitilessly poured. My God, why? Why can't this continuous bloodbath stop? The latest wars in Lebanon, Bosnia and Rwanda, daily devour young hearts and minds, and the world watches speechlessly, shrugging its shoulders in unconcern or despair. The American and the French peace corps who had tried to help are pulling out.

I had hoped that by New Year's Eve 1995--five years before the end of our mushroom-war century, we would see the end of wars, and that the whole concept and practice of warfare would be abolished. But the tragedy of wars continues endlessly, with fresh corpses of civilians and soldiers added to the long list every day.

However, the new year brings renewed hope. I have arrived at the conclusion that if the people of the world desire it, they can stop the monster called war from existing among us. If we all rise together against it, we can one day soon, cross it out from our historical dictionary. We can handle war just as we did its distant relative "dueling," which has been banned from the earth forever. The argument that man is an aggressive animal who likes to kill is simply untrue. I have interrogated many soldiers throughout more than half a century who have gone through several abominable wars. They all said they had hated killing other human beings.

I decided that the solution can only come from us, the

people--let us each cry out with all our strength: I do not want my children to be killed! Eventually we will be heard. This terrible practice called warfare, the abominable arrangement--I'll put my children here, you'll put yours in front of mine--they'll kill each other, and only then we will arrive at a peace treaty--has to stop. It has to be terminated before the end of this century, and war has to be banished forever. Anyway, every war ends with a peace treaty, so why not start there? Let's have the negotiations and the peace treaty, before the mutual killing of our children, and not the other way around! Nuclear arms have rendered wars more absurd than ever. In a nuclear war, no side wins. The only conqueror will be the total nuclear winter which will envelop the world. Those who will survive will envy the dead.

***

One important event in recent years strengthens my hope: I thank God that I have witnessed the signing of the peace treaty between Israel and Egypt, fifteen years ago, and have witnessed the beginning of the peace process between my people and the Palestinians, as well as a peace treaty between Jordan and Israel in October 1994, with the blessing and help of President Clinton. It is my greatest wish that peace will come soon over the Middle East and the whole world, creating goodwill bridges between all neighbors. *Inshallah,* in God's will, I may witness this too.

***

Suddenly, Moses, stalwart and powerful, rises before me, his Ten Commandments in his strong, sinewy hands and flashes of lightning in his wise eyes. He silently points a fiery finger at the fifth commandment: "Thou shalt not kill!" My breath stops in my lungs and my heart flutters in joy. Moses nods his head appreciatively, then winks at me, smiling. I am submerged by joy and fulfillment; my life has not been in vain.

Writer Ada Aharoni is awarded
the Témoignage Prize by Judge Guillaume Guillaine

THEA WOLF:
THE WOMAN IN WHITE OF THE JEWISH HOSPITAL IN ALEXANDRIA

"Ada Aharoni is awarded the prestigious "Prix du Témoignage" (Testimony Prize), for her fascinating and previously unknown World War history of the Jewish Community in Alexandria, and the Arab-Jewish co-operation in saving Jews from the Nazi Holocaust through the Jewish Hospital." *The Judging Committee, Paris.*

The "Prix du Témoignage", for the French version of the book, was awarded by book publisher Le Manuscrit and The Huffington Post. It was chosen from 3000 books, by a prestigious Committee of fifteen judges. The book was translated into French (from English), by Michel Mazza, and promoted by the ASPCJE: The Association of Jews from Egypt in France. The Hebrew version of the book was published in January 2015 by Carmel publishing House, Jerusalem, titled:

Lo Lashav: Gibora be Alexandria.
לא לשווא: גיבורה באלכסנדריה.

Ada Aharoni

Théa Wolf
La femme en blanc
de l'hôpital d'Alexandrie
(1932 – 1947)

Préface de Robert Solé

Prix du Témoignage
Lauréate
1ère édition 2004

Collection Témoignage

Le Manuscrit
www.manuscrit.com

COMMENTS AND REVIEWS

THE WOMAN IN WHITE: AN EXTRAORDINARY LIFE

By *Ada Aharoni*

President *Shimon Peres*, who awarded Prof. Ada Aharoni "The President Peace Award", wrote about the first edition of the book: "THE WOMAN IN WHITE: AN EXTRAORDINARY LIFE, is a lesson in Peace for all time, a lesson in Action for all women and men, and a real model of peace between Jews and Arabs. I highly recommend it."

Members of the Committee of the Témoignage Prize wrote:

"A moving and poignant narrative of the crossing of several aspects of contemporary history – the rising of the 3rd Reich, the Nazi Holocaust, the highly -cultured Jewish Community in Egypt, and the formidable creation of the State of Israel."

"It is extraordinary that The Jewish Hospital in Alexandria, that served the Allied forces battling against Rommel in El Alamein, saved the lives of hundreds of wounded soldiers, due to Sister Thea who invented the first Blood Bank."

"Ada Aharoni succeeds to draw the reader into this part of history that was totally unknown. The perfect authenticity in Aharoni's moving style goes straight to the heart. The book is a great bowl of humanity and of hope for peace in the Middle East. A great talent and a great book recommended not only for academia but also for the large public of all ages."

AN INSPIRING TRUE-LIFE STORY
Pejman Masrouri

In the book, *"Woman in White: an Extraordinary Life,"* author Ada Aharoni documents the inspirational real-life story of Thea Wolf, a German Jew who served as head nurse at the Jewish Hospital in Alexandria, Egypt, during World War II. The story of Thea's life is a journey through the wars and accompanying hardships of the 20th century. As a small child growing up in Germany she experienced the starvation of World War I and, though she miraculously escaped the horrors of World War II by being in Egypt, she lost 72 family members in the inhuman Nazi Holocaust. After her move to Israel in 1947, she bravely endured more wars, against Israel by her Arab neighbors, and steadfastly continued her efforts to help her fellow men.

Thea Wolf kept some records of her experiences, and in her interviews, she accurately related them to Prof. Ada Aharoni, who masterfully brought Thea's heroic actions to life in this unique book. Much of the story is set in Alexandria, Egypt, which was witness to a tumultuous tide of Jewish refugees who fled from Nazi Europe, attempting to escape the ravages of war and the horrible Nazi camps. The main recurring theme in this fascinating book, is how countless individuals were helped by Thea, who created a coalition of both Jews and Arabs, to save lives. The message that Jews and Arabs lived and worked together harmoniously, in Egypt, is a powerful one, and it generates hope that it is possible again today.

The book makes a strong anti-war statement, in sharing the poignant stories of refugees who were courageously saved by Thea. Thea, was much inspired by the words carved by Egyptian Queen Hatshepsut, "It is the wiser and stronger sovereign who makes peace, than he who makes war." Even after suffering from depression over the tragic fate of her extended family in Europe she did not succumb and instead she states, "I became a fighter again, on the side of life. I heard the call of humankind, imperious, irresistible, like a command…"

The world owes a debt to author Ada Aharoni who has brought in such a fascinating way, Thea Wolf's amazing life story to the public. As founder and World President of IFLAC: The International Forum for the Literature and Culture of Peace, she has devoted her life to building bridges of peace and eradicating violence and war. The French translation of this book was awarded the *"Prix du Témoignage"* (Testimony Prize) for its inspiring message of Arab-Jewish co-operation in Egypt, in saving Jews from the Nazi Holocaust, during the devastating World War II. This book should be made into a movie, with a good producer it can be a masterpiece!

***

MOTHER THERESA OF THE MIDDLE EAST
Dan Luiton

The Woman in White: An Extraordinary Life, by Ada Aharoni, tells the story about a Jewish German Nurse, called Thea Wolf, living and working in Alexandria, Egypt, at the Jewish Hospital in Alexandria, during World War Two. This book contains many tales about how this brave nurse succeeded to help Jews escaping from the horrors of Nazi Europe during World War Two, for the only motive of helping human beings. As a Mexican man, I rarely show any emotions, however, this was the first book which made me cry, on seeing she saved so many people who were destined to die.

At the beginning, the book seemed to be a common story about a Jewish girl who wanted to become a nurse, in a conservative society, who then went to Egypt, to found the school for nurses and to be the Head Nurse at the Jewish Hospital in Alexandria. Then, when she started talking about all the stories of her patients, I as a reader could not stop reading. The stories were so involving, and some even made me cry of happiness that those refugees who were destined to die were saved by her. One of the stories, that was not about the Nazi Holocaust, which also moved me so much, was "The Night of the Staircase", a story about a mother that had just given birth to a beautiful baby girl and yet was in deep sadness. She was sad because her husband forced her to stop working, because now she was already a mother. She did not want to stop working, because when she was young her mother couldn't continue her career as a pianist, because her husband told her to stop working, and

Emily didn't want to end like her mother. However, she did succeed to go back to her work after all because that was her joy, and she succeeded to make her husband understand that. This story moves me in particular because my mom was forced by my dad to stop working when she gave birth to her first son, my elder brother. Yet, she succeeded to go back to work twenty years later. I can relate to Emily because my mom like her, was so deeply sad because she couldn't work. However, it is something common in our culture, that women have to submit to their husbands. Even though my mom had a degree and my dad did not have one, she had to stop working. The author, Ada Aharoni, was right when she shows that women should have the equal right to work too. Why is this backward cultural idea that women should not work still exist? Women of course, should work if they want to, just like the men! I think this story in addition of the story of my mother, has made me a strong supporter of feminism. The most moving story of all in the book was THE ASTOUNDING PANCHO EPISODE, about four Czecho-slovakian Jews who tried to save their friends that were ship-wrecked on an abandoned island. Four hundred Czecho-slovakian Jews tried to escape the horrors of Nazi Europe, in an old ship, but the ship started sinking and they landed on the nearest desert island, somewhere in the Mediterra-nean. Four young Jews left the island on a raft to look for help for their friends and relatives. They were sailing for two days without water or food until they were picked up by a British war ship who thought they were German spies. When they got to Alexandria, the heroic head nurse, Thea

Wolf, tried to help them. She went to the British forces in Alexandria and told them the sad story of the *Pancho* ship. They sent two planes to look for the four hundred stranded refugees, but did not find any island with shipwrecked people. An Italian warship had fortunately spotted and saved them. The captain's name was Carlo, who took them all aboard and fed them, and taught them a little Italian. He told them he would take them to Sicily, where they would be safe if they did not say that they were Jews. They found work in Sicily and stayed there safely all through the war years.

***

Half a century later, when Ada Aharoni published the book NOT IN VAIN - AN EXTRAORDINARY LIFE, which was the first short edition of this book, and which contained this story, someone by the name of Abraham, called her and told her that he was one of those Jews from the Pancho, stranded on the island, and he reported to her the story of how they were saved.

The story of the Pancho does not end there; the survivors of the Pancho from all over the world, met in the congress which Thea and the mayor of Jerusalem organized, and they came with their children and grandchildren to feast the anniversary of their rescue. They were all delighted to meet with each other, it was so moving that they were able to find each other after so long. The reason I love the story is because there could be good and kind people even if they are enemies. In this case it was a good hearted Italian captain by the name of Carlo.

It is a unique story which tells another side of World War Two that needs to be written down in the book of history. For this reason, and because this excellent book is so very well written, I think this biography of Thea Wolf – The Mother Theresa of the Middle East, should be read by all and it will enrich all, as it so much enriched me on all levels!

I WAS SO TOUCHED BY THIS BIOGRAPHY OF THEA WOOLF'S LIFE!
Helen Grover

This wonderful book gently draws us into the life of Thea Woolf and into the world of this Jewish nurse who lived and worked in Alexandria, Egypt during World War II. She was born in Germany and trained to be a nurse there. She then served as a nurse in the Jewish hospital in Alexandria for many years. Being in Egypt before and during the war years not only saved her life but also thrust her into a leading role of helping Jewish refugees who came to or through Egypt in their attempt to escape the horrible Nazi Holocaust. The author, Ada Aharoni, masterfully relates several stories of people who took part in this fight to save so many lives, under the brave organization and leadership by the heroic Thea Woolf. These stories are both hopeful and uplifting, and so different from the usual tragic stories of the Holocaust.

In this fascinating book, Ada Aharoni reveals to us that Muslims and Egyptian Jews, under Thea's wise leadership, worked together for the cause of saving threatened lives. For these dedicated and caring people, saving human lives was more important to them than any religious differences. This book should be made into a film, it would be a fantastic one!

A FASCINATING BOOK
Rachel Newton, 15 years old

Wonderful book, easy to read even if you are a young person and even if English is not your mother language.

Once you start this book you don't want to leave it. A lot of great stories which captivated me. It taught me a lot about historical events of World War 2, which I did not know anything about, though we studied World War II at school. Very good example of a sincere cooperation between Jews & Arabs to save lives from Nazi Europe.

This is a must book for all teachers and all youngsters, and not only for adults. It will add important, hopeful and fascinating knowledge and enjoyment to all.

ABOUT THE AUTHOR

POET ADA AHARONI

Prof. Ada Aharoni was born in Cairo, Egypt, and she left with her family, during "The Second Exodus" of the Jews from Egypt. She now lives in Haifa, Israel. She is a writer, poet, sociologist and film producer, whose works have won international acclaim. She believes that communication, literature and culture, can help in healing the urgent ailments of our global village, such as war, conflict and poverty - by creating cultural bridges of understanding, harmony and peace among people and nations. The themes of peace and conflict resolution, as well as the recognition of the power of women as a great potential and ally of peace, are major ones throughout her works.

She has published thirty-three books to date, which have been published in several languages, including: English, Hebrew, French, Arabic, Spanish, Russian, Chinese, Portuguese and Vietnamese. She studied at London University, where she was awarded an M. Phil. Degree on *Henry Fielding*, and at the Hebrew University in Jerusalem, where she was awarded a Ph.D. in English Literature, on Nobel Laureate *Saul Bellow and his Introspective Fiction*. Ada's Award – winning historical novel, *The Second Exodus*, of the Jews from Egypt, was recently republished in a larger edition with the title, *From the Nile to The Jordan*, and it is a Bestseller on www.amazon.com. Among her published books are: Historical Novels, Biographies, History, Sociology, Middle Eastern Literature and History, Children's adventure books, and ten collections of poems in Hebrew, English, French, Arabic, Chinese, etc. and two books of translations of Israeli poetry, including Shin Shalom's *New Poems*. Two of her new collections of poems: *New Israeli Poems, a*nd *Pomegranates*, appear on www.amazon.com Kindle.

Ada Aharoni is the Editor-in-Chief of the IFLAC Anthology: *Anti-Terror and Peace*, as well as of the Anthology: W*aves of Peace d*edicated to the memory of the Israeli Peace Leader Yitzhak Rabin. She is the editor-in -chief of the Literary Magazines, *Galim: Iflac Waves* (1987-2017), and the electronic journal: IFLAC DIGEST on the Internet. Ada Aharoni is the recipient of several prizes and awards, among them are: The British Council Award, the Keren Amos President Award, the Haifa and Bremen Prize, The World Academy of Arts and Culture Award, the International Gold Crown of World Poets Award, the Rachel Poetry Prize, the "Merit Award," of HSJE: The Historical Society of the Jews of Egypt, awarded to her for her intensive research of the history and culture of this remarkable community. She received the "Peace Prize," by President Shimon Peres, and she was also awarded the title of "Honorary Citizen of the City of Haifa." The French translation of her book: "The Woman in White: An Extraordinary Life," received the "Prix du Témoignage », presented by Judge Guillaume Guillaine, representing the 15 members Jury Committee.

Ada Aharoni is the Founding President of IFLAC: The International Forum for the Literature and Culture of Peace (founded in Haifa, Israel, in July 1999). She was the Deputy Director of the Hebrew Writers Association in Israel, and the Head of its Foreign Relations Committee. She lectured in the Department of English Literature at Haifa University, and in the General Studies department of the Technion in Haifa. She has been invited as Visiting Lecturer at several American, and European universities, and as Keynote Speaker at Congresses and Conferences around the world.

Ada Aharoni lives on beautiful Mount Carmel in Haifa, Israel, where she writes and continues her peace research and activities, in the quieter moments of a busy literary, academic, and family life.

BOOKS BY ADA AHARONI

1. Whispered Thoughts - Haifa Publications, Haifa, Israel, 1970.

2. Poems from Israel - Outposts, Surrey, England, 1972.

3. Poems from Israel and Other Poems - Berger Publications, Pittsburgh, PA, 1974.

4. Metal and Violets - Eked, Tel Aviv, Israel, 1978.

5. From the Pyramids to Mount Carmel - Eked, T.A., Israel, 1979.

6. The Second Exodus: A Historical Novel - Bryn Mawr, PA, 1983. ISBN: 0-8059-2862-6. Library of Congress Catalog Card No. 82-90872.

7. Thea: To Alexandria, Jerusalem and Freedom - Bryn Mawr, PA, 1984. ISBN: 0-8059-2922-3. Library of Congress Catalog Card No. 84-91127.

8. Shin Shalom: New Poems - A Bilingual Edition, edited and translated from Hebrew to English by Ada Aharoni - Eked: Tel Aviv, 1985. ISBN: 965-90139-4-9.

9. Saul Bellow: A Mosaic, ed. Ada Aharoni, G. Cronin and L. Goldman; Peter Lang, N.Y., N.Y., 1992. ISBN: 0-8204-1572-3.

10. Selected Poems from Israel - Lachman, Haifa, 1992. ISBN: 965-90139-5-7

11. A Song to Life and to World Peace, ed. A. Aharoni, Mike Scheidemann et al. Posner and Sons, Jerusalem, 1993. ISBN 965-219-013-6.

12. From the Nile to the Jordan - Tamuz, 1994, M.Lachman, 1997. ISBN: 965-90139-0-6.

13. Peace Flower: A Space Adventure - Lachman, Haifa, 1994, 1996. ISBN: 965-90139. Ladybug Press, Ca., published a Spoken Book Taped Edition 1999.

14. Memoirs from Alexandria: Not in Your War Anymore - Hatikhon, G. Farah, Shfar-Am, 1997. ISBN: 965-90139-2-2.

15. Galim Literary Magazine, nos 1 - 8, edited Ada Aharoni - Tammuz, Tel-Aviv 1985- 1996.

16. Waves of Peace: In the Memory of Yitzhak Rabin, Galim 8, edited Ada Aharoni and Judith Zilbershtein, Hatichon: Shfaram, 1997. ISBN 965-222-774-9.

17. Peace Poems, A Bi-lingual Edition - Preface by M. Fawzi Deif, Cairo University, M. Lachman, Haifa, 1997.

18. Not In Vain: An Extraordinary Life - Ladybug Publishing House, California, 1998. ISBN 1-889409-18- (pbk)

19. Lirit: Poetry Israel, Founded and Edited by Ada Aharoni, Electronic Magazine on Internet, the Hebrew Writers Association, Agudat Ha-Sofrim Ha-Ivrim,Tel Aviv, no. 1- 1997, no.2 - 1998.

20. Horizon: Pave Peace, Online Magazine, nos.1 - 5. IFLAC- IPRA, 1996 - 2003.

21. Metal et Violettes: (In French), Characteres, Paris, 1996.

22. Du Nil Au Jourdain: (In French), Stavit, Paris, 2002.

23. You and I Can Change the World: Toward 2000, Micha Lachman, *Haifa, 1999.*

24. Women Create A World Beyond War and Violence, Micha Lachman, Haifa, 2002.

25. Three E-Books and C. D's: 1. You and I, 2. Peace Flower, 3. Women Creating A World Beyond War, Rowe Publications, England, 2003.

26. Selected Poems: Bilingual, Chinese – English, The Milky Way, Hong Kong, 2002. ISBN 962-475-288-5.

27. Woman in White, Micha Lachman, Haifa 2005. (in Hebrew).

28. Nearing of Hearts: A Historical Novel on the Jews of Egypt, Gvanim, 2007.

29. Rare Flower: Collection of poems dedicated to my departed daughter Tali , Dignity Press, USA, 2011.

30. Not in Vain, in Hebrew, Carmel Publications,

Jerusalem, 2014. (and in French, Paris)

31. IFLAC ANTHOLOGY on Anti-Terror and Peace, Amazon KDP, Kindle, 2016.

32. Zer Tvoua – A Garland of Wheat, Gvannim, 2017.

Articles and Interviews: A *hundred and sixty of Ada Aharoni's articles were published in professional journals and magazines, from 1967 - 2016.*
She was interviewed on her works, on IFLAC and on her life, on numerous media interviews in Israel and international media (1980 - 2017).

Robert Nissenson, Yigal Alfassi, Shoshia Beeri – Dotan, and Eden Rabin, composed music for Ada Aharoni's poems. *They are sung by Revital Levanon, Anat Yagen, Shoshia Beeri-*Dotan and other singers, on the discs "A Green Week," "To Haim to Life," and "Rare Flower" (1999-2017).

Ada Aharoni's songs, videos and Interviews can be watched on YouTube, as well as her award -winning film: THE POMEGRANATE OF RECONCILIATION AND HONOR.

Dr. Ada Aharoni is the Founding President of IFLAC the International Forum for the Literature and Culture of Peace, and the Editor of the IFLAC Digest on the Internet.

For more information about her and her work and projects, please visit the sites below:

The IFLAC Blog: www.iflac.wordpress.com
See Ada Aharoni on Wikipedia in English and Hebrew.

Ada Aharoni's books and e-books can be ordered at:
www. amazon.com and amazon KDP Kindle.

Ada's Homepage in Hebrew:
adaaharonihebrew.wordpress.com
In English:
www.iflac.org
Email: ada.aharoni06@gmail.com
Phones: 0544404750, 0773202818

THREE PHOTOS OF THEA AND ADA

Ada Aharoni presents a present to Thea Wolf, her book PEACE FLOWER, telling her "You are yourself Thea a true Peace Flower!

Thea and Ada with Ethiopian pupils, who were fascinated by Thea's extraordinary story and life!

Thea Woolf and Ada Aharoni

End

25281729R00158

Printed in Great Britain
by Amazon